CRITICAL
COUNTRYSIDE

The idyllic countryside still weaves a spell in many an advertising campaign. How long before it really is just a myth?

The reality as painted by Rex Whistler in the 1930s. The Vale of Aylesbury

CRITICAL
COUNTRYSIDE

JOHN BLUNDEN AND GRAHAM TURNER

BRITISH BROADCASTING CORPORATION

This book is based on the Open University television series *The Changing Countryside* first shown on BBC 2 in the spring of 1985 with repeat broadcasts beginning in September and March of each year up to and including the spring of 1988.

The programmes are part of the Open University course *The Changing Countryside* produced in association with the Countryside Commission. Full details of this may be obtained by writing to ASCO, The Open University, PO Box 76, Milton Keynes MK7 6AN.

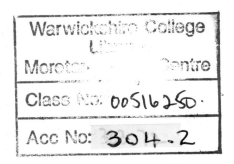
Published by the
British Broadcasting Corporation
35 Marylebone High Street
London W1M 4AA
ISBN 0 563 20318 8
First published 1985
© Open University &
British Broadcasting Corporation 1985
Set in 11/14 pt Imprint and
Printed in England by
Chorley & Pickersgill Ltd, Leeds

Contents

Introduction

W. G. Hoskins, in his pioneer work on the making of the English landscape, has written that:

> Since 1914, every single change in the landscape has either uglified it or destroyed its meaning, or both. Of all the changes in the last two generations only the great reservoirs of water for the industrial cities of the North and Midlands have added anything to the scene that one can contemplate without pain.[1]*

Such sentiments have also been echoed by Nan Fairbrother in her standard work *New Lives, New Landscapes*, though she embraces not just the landscape but all that constitutes the countryside. She wrote:

> To many of us in Britain, our countryside is the most beautiful landscape in the world; . . . [it has] evolved as a varied and harmonious whole by a long living together of man and nature in a gentle climate. But the modern world is now destroying this countryside inherited from the past; exploding the towns, swamping the villages, tearing up the farmland and spattering the old harmonious landscape with alien intrusions . . . With a few heartening exceptions, this is true everywhere . . . and it is profoundly depressing. But in another generation it will be disastrous, for by then the changes will have spread to every mile of our highly populated island.[2]

These two views of what has been happening to our countryside in the past ten years have been widely taken up by the media and have found expression in the large number of organisations given over to rural conservation and the regular pitched battles that take place at planning inquiries and elsewhere between those who wish to resist change to their environment and those who want to undertake new development forms. Indeed, an increasing body of opinion, both expert and lay, would suggest that where landscape is concerned the processes of evolution have given way in the twentieth century to the crude manufacture of landscapes which destroy and replace the older forms.

The debate which has taken place over these issues, conducted essentially in popular terms and in the language of confrontation, has been notable for the amount of heat produced and the lack of light illuminating the key issues.

See references on page 189.

The time is therefore right for a contribution which attempts an appraisal of the countryside of England and Wales, how it has evolved, what is happening to it now, and what sort of future we should envisage for it. It is just these objectives that this book attempts to meet in an informative and entertaining way with its main arguments conveyed primarily through an investigation of a number of distinctive rural areas of England and Wales.

A Suffolk landscape

Picture Credits

Chapter 1

Change and the Countryside

A recent opinion poll asked a cross-section of the public what it considered to be the most urgent problems facing Britain today. A very substantial majority thought the state of the economy to be of greatest significance, but, surprisingly, running a close second was the problem of the destruction of our traditional countryside. There is no doubt that there is widely publicised concern about this; indeed those with a particular interest in the protection of the landscape have been particularly outspoken. In 1976 Lord Henley, as Chairman of the Council for the Protection of Rural England, detailed the dangers of losing over a hundred square miles of rural land a year 'to roads, reservoirs, minerals, houses, schools, universities, factories, out-of-town shopping centres, new towns and so on, an area as big as Berkshire every five years', adding to this his doubts about the capacity of what remains not only to accommodate agriculture, but to handle the 'remorseless pressure for the use of land for recreation'.

More recently, emphasis has moved to the destructive potential of modern farming with polemicists like Marion Shoard, in her powerfully argued *Theft of the Countryside*,[3] stating categorically that the landscape of England is 'under sentence of death'. The executioner is not the industrialist or property speculator; instead it is 'the figure traditionally viewed as the custodian of the rural scene, the farmer'. She concludes that a new agricultural revolution is under way aided by new forms of farm technology, numerous production subsidies and assisted by a whole range of fertilisers and pesticides. 'If allowed to proceed, unhindered, it will transform the face of England.'

Lest such views seem representative of the special pleading of a vociferous minority attempting to sway the public to support the conservationist cause, even the more objective and cautious Nature Conservancy Council in 1984 presented an alarming account of what it calls 'the disappearance of the traditional British landscape at the hands of modern farming'. It speaks of the loss over the last thirty-five years of most traditional meadows, downlands, wetlands and lowland heaths. In England and Wales in this period, but more particularly at an accelerating pace in the last decade, ninety-five per cent of herb-rich meadows have gone, a quarter of the hedgerows and twenty-four million hedgerow trees. Over fifty per cent of lowland heath, the home of rare birds, flowers and reptiles, has been ploughed and planted, often with regimented rows of conifers. Fens and bogs have also disappeared, drained for agriculture or polluted by fertilisers. Only three per cent of the field system remains untouched by modern agriculture, leaving intact the ecosystems of traditional grasses and wild flowers. The destruction is greatest on the chalk downlands. Here eighty per cent of what were sheep-grazed pastures have been ploughed up for cereal production or 'improved' by being sprayed with fertilisers and weed-killers to encourage the grass at the expense of the flowers.

Indeed, at a personal level, many of us who love a particular tract of land in lowland Britain might be aware of such changes and could echo Richard Mabey's recent and heartfelt account of the fate of a Chiltern valley he has known since childhood. What he describes in his book *The Common Ground*[4] as 'a compact medieval landscape of ancient woods, hedges and pastures flanking the sides of a shallow river valley' had by 1980 changed out of all recognition. 'Not far short of half the hedges had been grubbed out. A thirty-acre primrose copse was cleared for wheat . . . As for the river this had disappeared underground and the hollow oaks and ashes that lay along it had

been felled!' He concludes, 'One spring I found the sheep pastures where I used to pick mushrooms covered with unfamiliar white granules and within a few years not only had the mushrooms vanished but the cowslips as well.' Only in the upland areas of England and Wales, a rather more robust landscape, have the changes that have taken place been more subtle and less ubiquitous – a stone wall taken away or allowed to fall down; a stream culverted; a new farm road built to replace an old stone track; or at most, a marshy piece of rough pasture drained, fenced, ploughed and reseeded. Even here, though, the enclosure and so-called 'improvement' of thousands of acres of Exmoor pasture is an indication of the extent to which Marion Shoard's 'new agricultural revolution' has imposed itself upon the landscape.

However, if the recent changes in our countryside appear to be dramatic as the result of newly-adopted farming practices, it would be wrong to imply that change has not occurred in earlier times or that until the last few years the landscape had enjoyed an immutable quality and had somehow stood apart from the social, economic and technological factors that have shaped the urban world. The reality is rather different. In the 6000 years that

Two contrasting Chiltern landscapes, scarcely five miles apart, illustrate how quickly today traditional landscape features can disappear, particularly as a result of modern farming methods. Turville *(left)* and Swyncombe *(below)*

have elapsed since the first Neolithic farmers began to make clearings in the great forests that clothed much of England and Wales, there has been what has been described as 'a centuries-long conversation between man and nature' in which the landscape has been constantly evolving. And, just as in the last few years the dialogue has become more earnest, resulting in a period of rapid change, so in the past it is possible to identify similar situations from time to time.

Perhaps the first major alteration in the countryside of England and Wales was achieved not by Neolithic farmers, whose impact must have been small, but by their Iron Age successors some 3000 years ago, whose use of metal rather than stone in the manufacture of their tools would have certainly speeded up the progressive removal of the tree cover. This must have occurred most rapidly during the Iron Age and later into Roman times in the upland areas and on some of the lighter soils. Yet even so the population was small and probably only about three per cent of today's farmland was under cultivation.

The impact of Anglo-Saxon invasions in the fifth and sixth centuries AD can be seen primarily on the lower ground and in the river valleys. With their particular type of plough they could work the heavier soils, and this led to the clearance of the lowland forests by a grubbing-out process and the establishment of a landscape of close-knit villages surrounded by large-scale open fields divided into a patchwork of arable strips and common pasture.

Many of these transformations are apparent from the Domesday survey of 1086 which, for the first time, offers detailed written evidence of countryside changes. Hitherto, ideas about how the landscape appeared in earlier periods rested primarily on the results of archaeological investigations. H. C. Darby,[5] the historical geographer, has used the evidence from Domesday to reconstruct many aspects of the eleventh-century landscape. Part of his work looks at changes in the forest cover of eastern England. A wider interpretation of Domesday shows that most of the villages existing today were in evidence by the middle of the eleventh century.

Other documents have enabled Darby to chart the changes in the forest cover through the medieval period. He has noticed fluctuations in the progress of woodland clearance as a result of war, pestilence and population decline or increase, and the growing destruction of the forests of the English Weald resulting from the needs of the iron-smelters and glass-makers for charcoal.

One result of the Arab conquests in southern Europe was the spread in the seventh and eighth centuries of the water-wheel as a source of power. Its effect on the landscape was twofold. Industrial processes at an early stage became linked to watercourses, particularly the fast-flowing streams of upland areas. Secondly, water was conducted to industry along canals,

The old medieval strip-field system shows up clearly from the air at Laxton, Nottinghamshire

conduits, aqueducts and tunnels, whilst mill-ponds and mill-races were also constructed to control the water supply. Together with charcoal-burning (and its attendant activities of metal-smelting and glass-making), these were the major impacts that industry made on the countryside throughout the Middle Ages. In the eastern counties of England, land reclamation from the sea and inland water marsh and fen also became of increasing interest from the thirteenth to sixteenth centuries.

W. G. Hoskins in *The Making of the English Landscape* provides a good picture of the countryside of England and Wales as it had evolved by 1500, and it indicates, up to that year, just how slow the process of man-made change had been. The landscape by that time was almost completely taken up

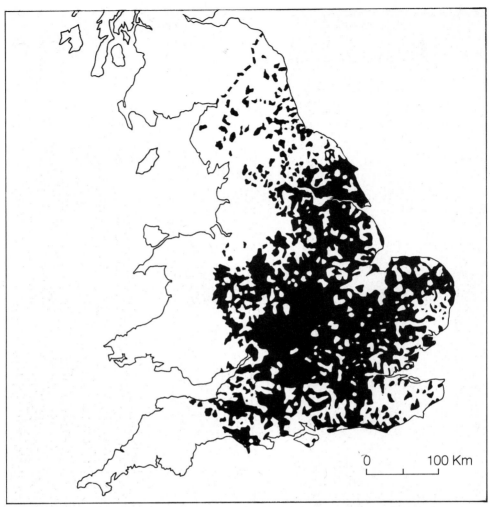

The maximum extent of the open-field system throughout England as identified by
C. S. Orwin in 1938

with agricultural land, woods, coppice, forest, parks or commons. As a result
of timber-felling for land clearance, for iron working, for building and for
fuel, agricultural land had increased to nearly fifty per cent, much of which
was under pasture. Towns were small, dispersed and hardly conspicuous.
Very few were centres in which manufacturing workshops played any major
role; indeed industrial activities were still small and rare. Many villages had
disappeared not only as a result of the Black Death but also because of the
enclosure of land and the rise of sheep farming in the thirteenth century.
Those villages that remained showed signs of increased prosperity and
growth, and country houses with their attendant formal gardens were
becoming features of the landscape.

More evidence of the past seen from the air: the site of a village (Lower Ditchford, Gloucestershire) probably wiped out either by the Black Death or by clearance to make way for sheep pasture

It is through the formality of such sixteenth-century gardens that we are able to observe for the first time, in any real sense, the attitudes of contemporary peoples towards their environment. Man's impact upon his surroundings still remained so marginal that the wilderness seemed all pervasive. Therefore beauty was perceived to lie only where order had been imposed on the landscape by the hand of man.

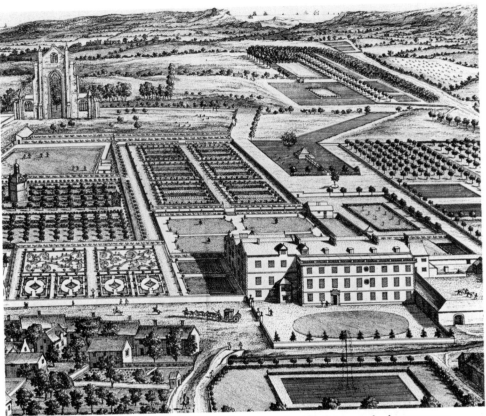

To the sixteenth-century mind 'natural' scenery had little appeal – beauty was perceived as an ordered mosaic of intricate gardens – Gisborough, Yorkshire

However, in the two hundred and fifty years or so up to the beginning of that period we call the 'Industrial Revolution', man's activities were to play an increasing role in shaping the landscape at large. Textile manufacture and glass-making developed from domestic crafts to become factory industries and their furnaces had a considerable impact on the countryside of the Midlands.

But, without doubt, it was the beginning of coal-mining on a large scale that had the greatest impact on the countryside. By 1650 severe deforestation made this imperative. Further expansion of the iron industry would have been impracticable had it not been able to move from the Weald and the Forest of Dean to the coal seams of South Wales, Shropshire and the Midlands. By 1660 Britain was producing five times as much coal as the rest of the world. But the level of man-made environmental change brought about by these activities was as nothing compared with what was to follow after 1740.

Until then, changes in the landscape can certainly be described as a steady

By contrast with the formality of the sixteenth-century garden, this view of Stourhead shows the eighteenth-century fashion for 'natural' garden landscaping

progression only disturbed by temporary fluctuations. The population had increased by fifty per cent in each century except for the reversals caused by the Black Death. All over the country, farming had spread to less profitable land. In England the old feudal organisation of the land had decayed and with it the open-field system which was gradually and patchily giving way to enclosed farms and fields. Everywhere, woodlands had diminished.

The Industrial Revolution was not an overnight phenomenon. It was a prolonged period in which the move towards industrial processes gradually gained momentum and in which the economy was transformed from an agrarian base to one much more dependent on manufactured goods. From the point of view of rural change, the Industrial Revolution probably had a more profound effect than anything since the agrarian revolution of the Neolithic cultures.

The impact of the revolution, exemplified through the introduction of new methods of spinning and weaving within the context of the factory system, was to be seen in the valleys of the Pennines where water power was available to drive machines. Mills, built seven or eight storeys high, eventually became a prominent feature, together with the workers' houses which surrounded them. But primarily, the Industrial Revolution was to rely on new sources of fuel and supplies of metal, with the massive development of a factory system closely related to the coalfields.

The availability of new steam engines to improve the efficiency of coal-mining, both in terms of haulage and ventilation, enabled mining to go deeper, and with this came increased quantities of waste shales etc., that were to become a pronounced and sterile landmark wherever this activity was pursued. The introduction of improved motive power which brought with it greatly increased output also caused an elaboration of pit-head apparatus: iron winding gear, frames and wheels, boiler chimneys, engine houses, water ponds, stock piles and tramways, all of which had considerable environmental impact at local level.

The working of metallic minerals in terms of change was, in certain cases, equally spectacular, though these were confined to specific areas. Certainly in the Cornwall of 1840, the 250 active tin mines created an extensive industrial landscape. Of more general importance than tin at the time was the development of a new technology with respect to the smelting and working of iron. The commercial casting of iron, using coal, by Abraham Darby at Coalbrookdale certainly achieved dramatic environmental change. However, it was particularly the discovery of how to convert cast iron to wrought iron,

Coal-mining, from its modest beginnings, transformed many areas of the country-side into the classic industrial landscape. Wallsend Colliery, Northumberland

An aquatint based on de Loutherbourg's 'Coalbrookdale by Night', described as 'a sublime representation of the furnaces of Bedlam' – a word to which the growth of industrialisation was to give new meaning. Interestingly, the original painting was included in de Loutherbourg's 'Romantic and Picturesque Scenery of England and Wales'. (Coalbrookdale, Salop)

the invention of cast steel and the use of hot-blast air to treble the output of furnaces, using not only coke but other coal fuels, that had even greater impact on the landscape. Iron foundries sprang up all over coalfield areas with their attendant large vertical blast furnaces, tall chimneys, engine houses and heaps of waste blast-furnace slag bringing even greater change to areas as diverse as the Yorkshire Moors, the Midland Plain and the valleys of South Wales.

The large increases in population which occurred at the same time as the Industrial Revolution resulted in greatly-increased demands for many things, one of these being pottery. This led to the development and rapid growth of the china clay workings of Lee Moor and Hensbarrow in the south-west of England, but fuel requirements helped confine pottery manufacture to the coalfields of the Stoke-on-Trent area, where other chemicals essential for glazing the pots were also available.

Where textiles were concerned, the major technological advances which had given rise to the factory system were now no longer confined by water power, and development continued mainly in the towns. The number of cotton mills in Manchester rose from two in 1782 to fifty-two in 1802. It was not, however, until the last quarter of the nineteenth century that the woollen industry became both mechanised and urbanised to a similar degree.

It was the rapid growth of the textile industry, once coal had become the motive power, that also gave a fillip to the development of chemical production for bleaching, colouring and, later, the printing of fabrics. The mining of the basic raw materials of the chemical industry (mainly salt) was not without its impact, particularly in such areas as Cheshire where considerable surface subsidence occurred from brine pumping. The manufacture of such chemicals in the open air caused the disfiguring of the landscape by the dumping of toxic wastes, the pollution of rivers by water run off from these dumps, and the destruction of vegetation as a result of fumes given off in chemical processing. So serious was the damage caused by hydrochloric acid being released into the air from the Leblanc soda-making process that in Britain the Alkali Act of 1863 was introduced to control its worst effects on the countryside.

Much as the developing processes of manufacture caused environmental change, so did the means by which its raw materials and products were carried about. Canals were not unusual in 1760 in England and Wales, but, as the first transport servant of the Industrial Revolution, the network was greatly extended in the following ninety years by some 4800 kilometres (nearly 3000 miles). Once constructed though, the impact of canals on the

Once the boisterous 'navvies' had finished their work, the canals often made an almost genteel contribution to the landscape – Rolle Canal, Torrington, Devon

countryside was rather limited as their routes tended to follow contour lines and thus blend into the landscape. Only in the Midlands can they, by their very concentration, have had a significant impact on the countryside. Similarly, the development of better roads after the middle of the eighteenth century to serve the needs of industry can hardly have had much effect since it was more a matter of improving their surface than driving new routeways. This was to be the prerogative of the railway builders after 1825; but even here, though the initial building of embankments and digging of cuttings were notable features of the landscape at first, these were soon colonised by plantlife and merged with the countryside. Only the more obviously man-made features such as the 25,000 railway bridges constructed between 1830 and 1860 remained as major indicators of change, whilst the large station buildings and termini were rapidly enveloped by the growing urban fabric of industrial towns.

The changes in rural England and Wales wrought by the Industrial Revolution were indeed remarkable. John Britton, writing in 1850, said of a journey through the Midlands:

From Birmingham to Wolverhampton, a distance of thirteen miles, the country was curious and amusing though not very pleasing to eyes, ears or taste. For part of it seemed a sort of pandemonium on earth – a region of smoke and fire filling the whole area between earth and heaven amongst which certain figures of human shape – if shape they had –

Saltash Bridge. The building of Brunel's masterpiece over the river Tamar. The rich tin and copper mines of Cornwall were soon accessible by rail

Though long abandoned, the old ridge and furrow patterns of the open-field system can still be seen in many English counties with the enclosures of the late eighteenth and early nineteenth centuries superimposed upon them, as here at Padbury in Buckinghamshire

were seen occasionally to glide from one cauldron of curling flame to another. The eye could not descry any form of colour indicative of country, or of the hues and aspect of nature, or anything human or divine. Although nearly mid-day in Summer, the sun and sky were obscure and discoloured. Something like horses, men, women and children occasionally seemed to move in the midst of the black and yellow smoke and flashes of fire, but were again lost in obscurity . . . The surface of the earth is covered and loaded with its own entrails, which afford employment and livelihood for thousands of the human race.[6]

Nevertheless, the impact of the Industrial Revolution was largely confined, leaving much of the countryside physically unchanged by it in any obvious sense. Indirectly, however, industrialisation made its mark. A larger population required a more efficient and productive agriculture, so new materials such as steel found their way into better ploughs, drills and reaping and threshing machines powered by steam engines. These pieces of agricultural hardware demanded bigger fields, whilst improved methods of husbandry (pioneered by Robert Bakewell of Dishley, Leicestershire, and Coke of Holkham, Norfolk) could be better practised in enclosed rather than open fields.

Indeed it was the abandonment of open fields and much of the land freely held in common that produced for the non-industrial countryside the most revolutionary influence since the breakdown of the manorial system of feudal times. If the writings of contemporary commentators are a guide, this change must have been felt as much as today's new agricultural revolution is in the late twentieth century. As John Clare, the great rural poet, wrote in 1821 of his native parish of Helpston in Northamptonshire:

> Ye fields . . . ye meadow blooms,
> Ye pasture flowers farewell!
> Ye banished trees, ye make me sigh –
> Inclosure came and all your glories fell.

Sixty years later, Flora Thompson in describing her childhood home of Lark Rise in north-east Oxfordshire could write of the ripening cornfields rippling to the doorstep of the cottages of her hamlet 'on an island in a sea of dark gold'. 'To a child,' she says, 'it seemed that it must always have been so.'[7] Yet the powerful memory of what had happened over half a century earlier remained strong in the minds of the people, for she reports that 'the ploughing and sowing and reaping were recent innovations. Old men could remember when the Rise, covered with juniper bushes, stood in the midst of a Furzy heath in common land and which had come under the plough after the passing of the Enclosure Acts.'

Developments in industrialisation and agricultural techniques had by the 1850s effected a considerable change in the appearance of rural England and Wales as well as in people's attitudes towards it. Now, for the first time, with the majority of the population living in the towns, came a true awareness of the hand of man upon the landscape. As areas of wilderness became rare, once the wastes had gone and were replaced throughout the lowlands by a chequerboard countryside of enclosed fields, the idea of beauty in the landscape came to be attached to the remoter and wilder countryside of the uplands. It was a feeling given much expression by the popular romantic poets such as Wordsworth and Byron.

If the industrial and agricultural revolutions which spanned the eighteenth and nineteenth centuries led to a considerable growth in man's capacity to effect changes in his surroundings, not least the countryside, they were only

As a response to growing industrialisation the Romantic wilderness became a popular vogue. Crummock Water, Cumberland

the forerunners of the even more fundamental and widespread alterations of the twentieth century. But whilst urbanisation in the nineteenth century had shown itself only in the development of crowded tightly-packed towns, the growing pressures of populations in the 1930s were coupled with higher living standards, cheap transport and a greater demand for personal space. This inevitably led to lower-density housing developments and a very considerable transfer of what had been farm land to urban uses, a transfer aided and abetted by a depression in the agricultural industry. Losses of such land in England and Wales reached 25,000 hectares (nearly 62,000 acres) a year in the mid 1930s. This rate of change was drastically reduced after the war, mainly as a result of the introduction of a statutory system of land-use planning controls. In addition, in at least ten areas of scenic attraction, these controls were supplemented through their designation as National Parks. In other areas, also of considerable landscape significance, the status of 'Area of Outstanding Natural Beauty' and 'Heritage Coast' have been applied to assist in their protection against development and to enhance their use for recreational purposes.

Apart from an increasing use of land for the extraction of minerals and the demands made upon rural areas by water collection and power production and transmission, by far and away the greatest single loss of land in the last twenty years in England and Wales has been the development of motor-ways. Every kilometre of motorway causes the development of at least $12\frac{1}{2}$

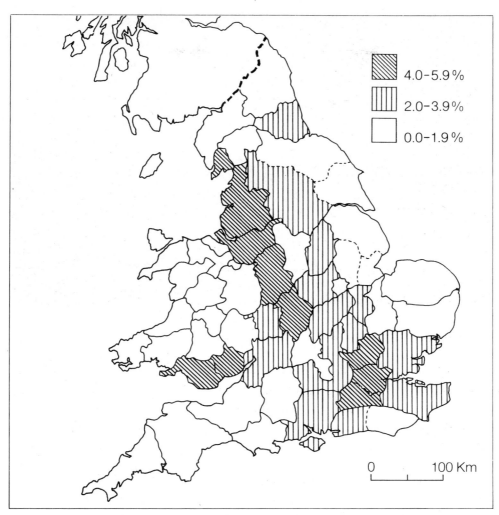

4.0–5.9%
2.0–3.9%
0.0–1.9%

0   100 Km

Transfers of agricultural land to urban use in England and Wales by counties, 1950–70 (after Champion, 1974).

hectares of land (that is, nearly 50 acres for every mile). Yet, even in spite of such voracious demands for land, only eleven per cent of the total area of England and Wales can be considered to be in urban use. Much is still given over to agriculture or a combination of agricultural and recreational pursuits.

On the agricultural land itself, the twentieth century has seen the dramatic impact of sophisticated and powerful farm machinery. Such machines have particularly encouraged a change, from a field size which was appropriate in an age of ox and horse power, to much bigger units of land. Indeed it has been estimated that nowadays a square field of about twenty hectares (around fifty acres) allows the most efficient use of field machinery. It is no small wonder then, that in those parts of the country whose climate is best suited to the

Small, irregular fields are ill-suited to the mechanised farming that developed after the Second World War. Contrast the field patterns around Beccles in Norfolk in 1945 (*above*) with those of 1970 (*right*)

production of cereal crops, agricultural landscapes have undergone the greatest change through the removal of hedgerows and the amalgamation of small fields into larger units. This has provided the additional significant bonus to the farmers of making available for productive purposes one hectare of land for every 0.88 kilometres of around two-metre-wide hedge removed (or nearly five acres for a mile of two-yard-wide hedge). In Britain in the period 1951–75, 80,000 kilometres (nearly 50,000 miles) of hedgerows were

removed. The effects on the countryside of such destruction is looked at in a later chapter.

Several studies have been undertaken of changes in the patterns of field boundaries. One of these, using aerial photography, has been applied to Norfolk, a county with a considerable area under cereals. Photographs taken near Beccles contrast the irregular field patterns of 1945, before the impact of fully-mechanised farming, with the situation for 1970. The later photograph shows that fifty per cent of the hedgerows, together with small woods and coppices, had been removed in the twenty-five-year period. A study of the maps of three parishes in Norfolk, Bradenham, Scarning and Shipdham (all

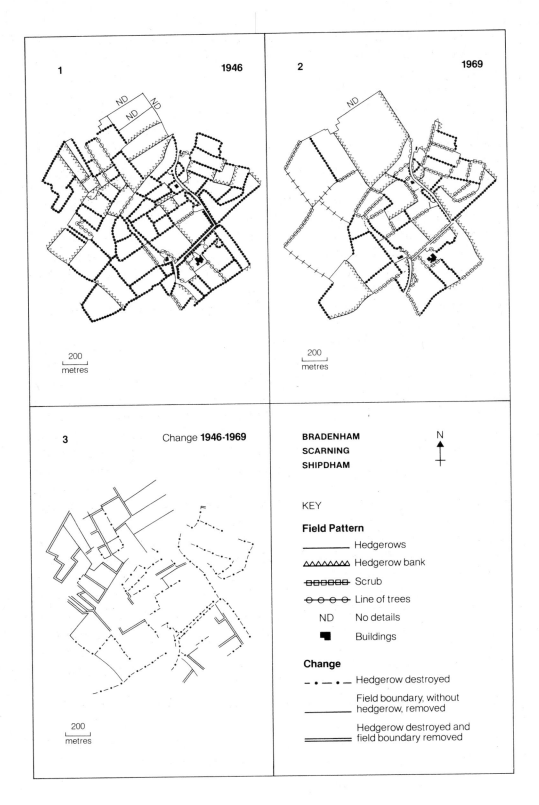

1   1946

ND ND ND

200
metres

2   1969

ND

200
metres

3   Change **1946-1969**

200
metres

BRADENHAM
SCARNING
SHIPDHAM

N

KEY

Field Pattern

———————— Hedgerows

△△△△△△△ Hedgerow bank

▭▭▭▭▭▭ Scrub

⊖ ⊖ ⊖ ⊖ Line of trees

ND   No details

◼   Buildings

Change

– • — • — Hedgerow destroyed

———————— Field boundary, without
               hedgerow, removed

════════ Hedgerow destroyed and
               field boundary removed

on heavier land than that near Beccles and thus traditionally less suited to cereal production), indicates clearly and in detail the magnitude of change over the same time span.

More recent figures for the county as a whole show that the overall hedgerow losses which were running at around fifty per cent in 1970 have now (1984) reached eighty per cent. Elsewhere in Norfolk the increasing preoccupation with cereal production is leading to the draining of 607 hectares (1500 acres) of Broadland. In other parts of lowland England similar examples can be quoted – in south Dorset alone half the prehistoric barrows of the Ridgeway have been ploughed up to the same end. Even upland areas, usually more resilient to change, have felt the impact of the new agricultural revolution. From 1954, when Exmoor was designated a National Park, through to 1975 it had lost twenty per cent of its open land to enclosure and so-called agricultural 'improvement'. Here, as elsewhere, not only has the appearance of the countryside altered in ways which are quite obvious, but habitats with unique associations of flora and fauna have been lost, according to the Nature Conservancy Council.

As well as affecting the appearance of the open country, recent agricultural developments, with their ever-increasing investment requirement and their substitution of capital for labour, have had an impact on the villages. Thus these, once the centre of agriculturally-based communities, are no longer so. Almost mirroring the loss of labour on the land and the departure of the farm worker from the village in search of other employment – usually in the towns – has been the growing influx to rural areas of those who once lived in towns. The decrease in the importance of distance as people's real incomes rose became even more important in the post-war period than it had ever been in the 1930s. This brought into the village the young and prosperous family. Aspiring to lead for self and family 'the good life', the head of household is prepared to commute daily to work in the nearest large town or in cities even further afield. At the same time, villages in the more scenically attractive areas have come to provide homes for the retired. More occasional visitors have also invested in country cottages as holiday homes. Village shops, once an essential part of a largely immobile agricultural population to whom they supplied the most basic needs, have been transformed into gift and antique shops if they have not been closed down altogether. Services of all sorts, whether they be the day-to-day or other welfare needs of country dwellers, have become more and more centralised in large towns. At the same time public transport has drastically declined leaving those without cars, notably

Left : The remorseless loss of landscape features is graphically illustrated by these contrasting maps of three Norfolk parishes. Such changes were typical of many parts of lowland East Anglia

Meanwhile in the Uplands open moorland has been steadily enclosed, to improve pasture for sheep-rearing. An Exmoor landscape

the old and the young, less and less able to move around. Their freedom of choice and quality of life, some would argue, has been seriously impaired.

We have tried in this first chapter to establish that although change in the countryside is not a phenomenon applicable only to this century, it is one of the periods when the rate and impact of change has been sudden and widespread. Moreover, the last decade or so has been particularly distinguished not only by a transformation of the social and economic fabric of rural communities but by agricultural practices that have transformed the landscape.

Indeed, as a result of government price support for a range of agricultural produce and the availability of grants for farm improvements, there has been a marked reduction in what the Nature Conservancy Council has called 'the rich variety of the traditional countryside'. But just as we have tried to show that in the past what people actually thought about the landscape was a crucial element in any discussion of what they wanted and expected from rural areas, this remains true today, perhaps even more so. To the middle-class car-owning newcomers to a village, it may represent the realisation of a dream of the perfect 'away-from-it-all' rural idyll. To the agricultural worker the same village may be home, but it is a home increasingly devoid of essential services and without any personal means of transport and one of growing isolation and expense. But even more important to this discussion is the attitudes people have towards the countryside beyond the village. Here the farmer, perhaps with a large acreage under arable production in East Anglia, may see in his landscape of hundred-acre fields that beauty which comes from the knowledge that what he admires from his farmhouse window is the outward expression of his efficiency and prosperity. But to the person wanting to use the countryside for recreation and leisure this same area may represent a featureless, bleak landscape devoid of trees, hedges, wayside brooks and ponds, all of which can give pleasure on a day's walk. To the conservationist it represents the ultimate in the destruction of natural habitats and one further example of the way the great variety of species is being diminished. All these varying views of what the countryside should be for frequently have to be accommodated by a single tract of land, a tract which may not merely be given over mainly to agriculture but possibly may have to serve the interests of forestry, minerals extraction or water collection. In such instances, questions as to how these different uses may harmoniously co-exist may be difficult enough. The situation is further complicated when it is realised that even individual attitudes towards the countryside are not fixed and may change with circumstances – even the most zealous agri-businessman from East Anglia may want a holiday on, say, Exmoor. Will he then want to see the open moorland enclosed and 'improved' for agriculture?

Change in the countryside is a complex issue which involves not only the changes themselves but our attitudes towards them. The countryside of Britain has to fulfil a myriad of needs for what is essentially a highly-urbanised population. Because all our needs, be they for food, housing or recreation, are greater today than ever before, it should not be surprising that changes are taking place in our environment faster than ever before. How we and the countryside can cope with this situation is something we look at in the following chapters.

Chapter 2
Scenic Setting

EACH year, many hundreds of thousands of visitors pour into the north-west corner of Wales, to enjoy themselves in a variety of ways amid the mountains, forests, moors and coastline of an attractive part of Britain's countryside. Most are aware that the greater part of the region is a designated National Park and therefore an area set aside for people's recreation and enjoyment. For many visitors, the association of 'beautiful' scenery with a National Park is complete; the designation of one is the definition of the other. Few would pause to consider just how recently this identification has come about and how, paradoxically, the creation of the Snowdonia National Park in 1949 heralded an era of unprecedented change in the landscape of Britain's officially most-protected countryside.

Observed from one of the many satellites that keep watch over activities on our planet, the strange ritual of a British Bank Holiday must appear as though a manic lemming-like urge has gripped the population and caused entire communities to assemble in vehicles of every ilk to surge towards the country's geographic periphery – as though they were either escaping some holocaust or were seeking some greatly sought-after treasure. Most certainly there seems to be a planned and efficiently executed pilgrimage to places which exert a most powerful attraction. But once there the behaviour pattern is more confused. Some climb to the tops of the most inaccessible mountains, others take to boats on the sea watched by thousands on the shoreline, others set off deep into forests, while others are dotted about the open moorlands that dominate the landscape. Such mass pilgrimages are a modern phenomenon.

It does seem extraordinary that it was not until 1639 that we had the first recorded ascent of Snowdon. This was made by one Thomas Johnson. He was a botanist who found 'our British Alps veiled in cloud', not an unusual occurrence in these parts. What is of interest, too, is his reference to the 'Alps'. Clearly he, and we might assume his contemporaries, had a better knowledge of Swiss mountains than those in Wales. The isolation of these mountains gradually began to break down when another visitor, Thomas Pennant in 1781, started a cult which attracted painters, antiquarians, poets and others of a scientific inclination. This interest, it is generally agreed, was part of the eighteenth-century Romantic movement which blossomed throughout the British Isles and Europe in the aftermath of the French Revolution.

William Wordsworth is credited by some with being the founder of conservation and through his writing the appreciation of 'natural' scenery gained the widest expression. Through his pantheistic beliefs, the seeing of God in nature, Wordsworth influenced generations: increasingly people saw in the mountains of Britain God's own country. Yet his philosophy was not a populist one. In his reaction to the building of the railway from Kendal into Windermere, Wordsworth condemned the prospect of hordes of visitors. The sublime beauties of nature, of the mountains and lakes were a cultivated passion, and above appreciation by the 'common mind'.

Is there no nook of English ground secure
From rash assault?

As well as the poets and scientists, came privileged travellers who were content to gaze upon the awe-inspiring grandeur of the mountain scenery and contemplate the sublime beauties of a new landscape far removed from the ordered uniformity of the English lowlands. It was a new idea to find this type of landscape attractive. Before the Romantic movement, travellers had found the area bleak, desolate and inhospitable. However, by the middle of the nineteenth century, the fashion for walking the hills was in full swing – George Borrow describes his ascent of Snowdon in 1854: 'We were far from being the only visitors to the hill this day. Groups of people, or single individuals might be seen going up or descending the path as far as the eye could reach.'[8] Borrow called his book *Wild Wales* and its title denotes the need felt by a growing mass of town dwellers to experience a wild unaltered landscape.

Ten years after Borrow's ascent of Snowdon, in the aftermath of the American Civil War, Abraham Lincoln signed an Act of Congress whereby the Federal Government ceded to the State of California the Yosemite Valley and Mariposa Grove of giant sequoias to be used as a public park 'inalienable for all time'. It was the first legislation to enable the ideal of the National Park to take root and it was one which fired the imagination of many on both sides of the Atlantic.

The American idea was to preserve for posterity vestiges of truly virgin territory which had escaped the great migration of people, industry and capital across the continent of North America. In of two generations, an almost unparalleled tract of wild country had been cleared, fenced and ploughed into settled productive land. The appropriation of areas of land for National Parks attempted to do for nature what the Indian reservations did for what remained of the indigenous population: to make an enclave of territorial museums away from the mainstream of change which was sweeping the country.

One doubts whether anyone in Washington DC consulted the Indian

The highest mountain in England and Wales, accessible by train for nearly 100 years – Wordsworth would have been aghast

---

Map 1 *Snowdonia*

The Ordnance Survey Map of part of the Snowdonia National Park illustrates how much the 'natural' landscape has been altered by man. The number of railways, planted forests, mine workings and ruins of all kinds shows the handiwork of successive generations.

population of Yosemite, and it is by no means certain that the native Welsh of Caernarvon and Merioneth were overjoyed to see their farms and villages subsumed as the Snowdonia National Park in 1949. Each piece of legislation was an imposition from outside the area concerned. It was an expression that certain areas of countryside had a value as an important resource to the nation as a whole.

The notion of National Parks was one we imported from the United States. In Britain the name was to be given a very different interpretation. The whole concept of what a National Park is, rests on certain assumptions and conjures up different meanings to different people. At its very heart are two important issues – the first is conservation of a particular landscape; the second is an implied guarantee of access to this protected countryside for those who wish to enjoy it. Ann and Malcolm MacEwen in their assessment of National Parks point to the confusion: 'In the UK the title National Park has misled visitors and native alike for more than thirty years arousing fears (among natives) that have little justification and expectations (among visitors) that it has not satisfied.'[9]

Let us deal with the visitors' expectations first. Unlike the Yosemite Valley or Yellowstone Park in the USA, very little of the landscape of Snowdonia could be considered wild or 'natural'. George Borrow's experience on the top of Snowdon or Eryri, to give its native Welsh name, seems familiar to most contemporary visitors. He was at pains to ignore on the summit 'a rude cabin in which refreshments are sold', and concentrate on the 'frightful precipices' or the view into the valley a mile below:

> . . . to the gazer it is at all times an object of admiration, of wonder and almost fear. We stood [Borrow was accompanied by his step-daughter, Henrietta] enjoying a scene inexpressibly grand. Peaks and Pinnacles we saw about us and below us, partly in glorious light, partly in deep shade. Manifold were the objects which we saw from the brow of Snowdon but of all the objects which we saw, those which filled us with most delight and admiration, were numerous lakes and lagoons which like sheets of ice or polished silver lay reflecting the rays of the sun in the deep valleys at our feet.

Borrow makes it clear what component of the view *he* enjoyed. It must have looked to him as it does to us at first, a very natural spectacle. But is this description truly accurate?

As far as we can tell, George Borrow would have seen precious little of the lakes and valley floors if the view he had witnessed had not been altered by thousands of years of man's interference. What a 'natural' view from Snowdon would look like we can only conjecture. Given the present-day climate, it seems likely the peaks would rise out of forests of oak and birch which would cover the area of the National Park up to a height of perhaps 650 metres (2000 feet). Above this, rough scrubby grassland would survive where a sufficient soil had developed and mosses and lichen would help clothe the bare rock or scree slopes. There would not be the many additional rock outcrops resulting from centuries of mining activities which litter the hillsides. In any event, most of the year, the view would be shrouded in mist and rain, if not lashed by ferocious storms. In this respect, the evocation of wilderness can arguably be more attributed to the weather than the landscape and, as such, the view of the real world may accord more with the 'desolate and inhospitable' school of thought which prevailed before the Romantics.

Away from the high peaks, a quest for anything approaching a natural landscape is even more difficult. Everyone has a preference even to the extent of believing in what is 'natural' and often where it has been made possible through the acquisition of enough land and money, we find attempts to change the landscape into an individual's conception of the ideal 'natural scene'. One commentator has described such a landscape:

> Perhaps the most spectacular examples of the influence of landowner-ship and economic practices on the outward appearance of a landscape may be seen along the balmy southern shore of Anglesey, facing the Menai Strait. Here a succession of estates occupies the coastline westwards from the Menai Bridge. Plas Llanfair, Plas Newydd, grandest and most famous of country houses, Plas Mona and Plas Coch have obliterated a landscape of medieval settlement and farming. . . . By the nineteenth century, this coastal site of high natural beauty, one of Britain's finest panoramas in which the changing colours and cloud-scapes of Snowdonia's mountains are viewed across the calm mirror of the Strait, was subject to the principles of 'landscaping' that were in vogue at that time. The estate of Plas Newydd together with the planted woodland, lawns and lakes of Vaynol Hall on the facing shore of the Menai Strait, together form a unique element among the landscapes of Britain where the subtle arts of man blend with the natural elements of sea, sky and mountains.[10]

Well, that is one assessment. In another part of Snowdonia, a landscape was being created in the nineteenth century, by forces which had nothing whatsoever to do with aesthetics but with economics. The wealth to transform the estate of Vaynol Hall had been generated by the Assheton-Smith family slate quarries in Nant Peris.

Now disused, the Dinorwic slate quarries provide one of the most striking examples of man's ability to change the natural scenery. An entire mountainside has been etched away in a staircase of galleries from where the characteristic blue slate of Nant Peris was carved out to roof thousands of

'The sublime arts of man and nature' is one description of the landscaped vistas of Snowdonia. From across the Menai Strait, Plas Newydd, Anglesey

The awesome disfigurement of an entire mountainside – the terraces of the disused Dinorwic slate quarry now conceal the turbines of an electric power station

Left : Inspiring grandeur or bleak desolation? A winter landscape in Snowdonia

terraced homes in the growing industrial cities. The contrast between this landscape of unashamed exploitation and the indulgence of the scenic estates along the Menai Strait points directly at the conflict in our values in looking at the countryside. Somehow the landscape which emerges from the economic necessities of society seems far inferior to the ideal of a perfectly harmonious landscape proffered by the painter or poet. It does seem at least arguable that our pleasure and appreciation of the appearance of the countryside can be as much influenced by what we have seen painted or visualised in verse and writings as by what we personally experience.

It was not only slate in vast quantities that the industrial cities took from the hills of Snowdonia. The need for even greater volumes of clean water led to the creation of large artificial lakes as reservoirs for water supply. Lake Bala and Vyrnwy were the forerunners of water catchment schemes which took many hectares of land. As features of the landscape, they remain aesthetically and politically controversial.

W. G. Hoskins singles them out as the only man-made features of the twentieth-century landscape we can contemplate 'without pain'; whereas to the purist, any artificial body of water must remain ill-at-ease with its surroundings. The decision must, as with so many other areas of landscape appreciation, be a subjective one. Suffice it to say that these reservoirs give further proof that such areas of the country, no matter how geographically remote they might be, could not escape the greedy, rapacious maw of the needs of towns and cities. The subsequent designation of National Park status also proved to give little 'protection' to the large-scale transformation of the countryside.

There is no better exemplar of this than the growth of the electricity supply industry in the post-war period. Some writers have commented waggishly that no self-respecting National Park is complete without a nuclear power station.

Leaving to one side the intractable debate on the rights and wrongs of nuclear power generation, it is still possible to argue in countryside terms that the decision to create a national super grid of power supply serviced by generating stations on the largest scale has been of unequalled effect on many areas of the British countryside. Any traveller on the east coast rail line from London to Edinburgh will not fail to notice this as the landscape of Nottinghamshire and Yorkshire slips by. Similarly, few can travel through the Oxford Vale without noticing the dominating presence of Didcot Power Station. The transmission lines for these giants are even more ubiquitous; one can hardly find a view in the country that is free of them. They also symbolise another revolution in so far as the almost universal supply of electricity has profoundly affected the limits on comfortable settlement in rural areas. It is hard to imagine the old workers' cottages of Snowdonia exercising quite such appeal as holiday homes if their town-based residents were still needing to carry the coal for the fire and the paraffin for the lamps.

As the income from slate quarrying and other mining activities in North Wales dwindled after the First World War, the major landowners looked for other enterprises. Forestry provided one possibility and soon the distinctive profile of coniferous plantations began to appear on the Welsh hillsides. Landowners attracted to this method of planting were reinforced by a new statutory body, the Forestry Commission, which began in 1920 the transformation of a great expanse of steep hillside and moorland around Betws-y-Coed into modern productive forest. This became the Gwydyr Forest. It was designated a forest park in 1937 and was eventually incorporated into the Snowdonia National Park in 1949.

Within this forest one can find vestiges of the previous forest which would have been the natural vegetation over the lower slopes of the area. These have now been overwhelmed by the planting of imported species of conifer such as spruce, larch, pine and Douglas fir. One can still see groves of Douglas fir close to Betws-y-Coed, the original seed for which was brought from Oregon. It seems somehow appropriate as a reinforcement for our importation of the concept of a National Park from the United States, that the Forestry Commission in planting these species created consciously or subconsciously a landscape more reminiscent of the wilderness of coastal sierras of California than the long-settled slopes of Snowdonia.

Today, any cursory look at the Ordnance Survey maps of North and Central Wales will reveal vast areas afforested. In the Dovey Forest above the still-active slate-mining village of Corris, we can see the kind of landscape that results. Here blocks of mature trees are interspersed with areas recently clear felled and other new plantings of young trees. The land is worked over systematically. Useful timber is cut out every thirty years or so with younger growth going to provide pulp for the voracious paper and packaging industry.

The plans for further afforesting large areas of the country are as impressive as they are controversial. No less than a third of the open moorland of the country is likely to be under conifers by the end of this century if present plans are carried out.

In the search for a natural landscape in Snowdonia, a part of Wales' open moorland is one possible contender. Millward and Robinson identify, 'Large areas of the headwater basin of Tryweryn, especially in the region known as Migneint, as exceptionally boggy and therefore trackless. Here is a wild landscape of open moorland with its rushes, cotton sedge and occasional tarns that has been left virtually untouched throughout history.'

The notion of wild landscape brings us back to the quest for that most intangible experience of a personal contact with nature.

The Yew, one of only three coniferous species native to Britain, shades the grave-yard at Maentwrog

The landscape of commercial forestry – this kind of countryside will become much more extensive in Upland Britain

The open moorland of the Migneint – an untouched landscape which can arouse strong emotional reactions. Much of this is soon to be forested

The call of the wild – Snowdonia. The right to roam is one we expect from any National Park – but our legal rights are few

For some it is the lure of the moors. Marion Shoard in her contribution to the book on *Valued Environments* attempts to define the appeal. She writes of the necessity to have countryside which appears not to bear the imprint of the works of man, which has openness, solitude and where one has the freedom to wander at will.

Some would argue the last attribute is the most important of all; the personal need for space and countryside can be fulfilled according to the individual's taste. The call of the wild may spring from a rugged seashore, desolate mud flats, lonely heath, precipitous crags or deep forest, even one that is coniferous. In any of these environments, the nub of the matter is access, which for the recreational needs of a large town-based population seems in recent years to have become concentrated on the National Parks.

So far, in looking at some landscapes in North Wales, we have not mentioned the most important influence by far on the appearance of the countryside: that of farming. Without the grazing of sheep and cattle, and cultivation of crops in favoured valleys, the entire area of the National Park would be woodland up to about 610 metres (2000 feet) in today's climate. Even in this relatively unrewarding agricultural environment, farmers throughout history have been the most pervasive influence.

Their interest today is often in conflict with the area's wider role of being designated a National Park. By its very title, it indicates a shifting balance between those who live and work in the countryside and those outside who see the region as a holiday area and an escape from their day-to-day environment.

There has been consistent opposition to National Parks by the Welsh National Farmers' Union, and in 1972 an attempt by the Countryside Commission to extend the National Parks by seeking a National Park designation for the Cambrian Mountains, 120,952 hectares (467 square miles) in mid-Wales, was not confirmed by the Secretary of State for Wales on grounds of unprecedented vigorous public opposition.

Ultimately we are faced with an insoluble problem with our National Parks. In England and Wales a population of around 50 million is located on a land base of about 15 million hectares (or just over 37 million acres). Inevitably, land has to be used for more than one purpose. So even if our National Parks consider their main objectives to be recreation and the conservation of the landscape, these cannot exist alone. No National Park in England and Wales can ever approach the National Park ideal as exemplified by Yosemite – for us agriculture and forestry, in particular, will have to have their place.

Yet in spite of this, should we really say that nuclear power stations, early warning systems, mammoth quarries, reservoirs, new motorways etc. are acceptable? One solution put forward by the Countryside Review Committee in 1979 (a group made up from civil servants within departments of government concerned with rural affairs) suggested a two-tier system of separately distinguished landscape areas. In one the quality of the landscape would be such as to suggest the complete exclusion of any activity incompatible with basic conservation ideals. In the other, the basic ethics of the National Park would remain the chief consideration, but with a greater freedom to embrace other forms of activity. These recommendations were not accepted by government although they were a compromise in the face of a hardline approach which would exclude all new developments from any part of a National Park. Advocates of such an approach have vociferously attempted to fight off all such incursions at public inquiries and although over a period of some thirty years they have frequently convinced the presiding inspectors they have notably failed to achieve any degree of success with successive Secretaries of State for the Environment or their predecessors.

Some would argue that a system which allows such a Minister of State the final say in these matters, even against the evidence, will inevitably find the countryside the victim of short-term political expediency. But perhaps it really says more about a general failure to appreciate the rural landscape as a truly valued resource.

Chapter 3
The Face of the Fells

THERE is no more celebrated area of upland landscape in England than the Lake District. Like so many areas of the country it is a spectacular geological miniature. It covers, in global terms, a microscopic part of the earth, yet it contributes a landscape of outstanding character. What features have contributed to this character, we look at in one lakeland valley.

The Hartsop Valley viewed looking north from the Kirkstone Pass

---

Map 2 *Lake District : Patterdale and Hartsop*
Dominated by Helvellyn the fells and lakes of this part of Cumbria are typical of the scenery which attracts millions of visitors. The intricate mosaic of becks and hills provide constantly changing vistas for walker and motorist alike. National Trust ownership in this area is extensive; in the Lake District National Park as a whole it amounts to over a quarter.

Hartsop forms an attractive 'self-contained' valley between the Kirkstone Pass in the south and Ullswater in the north. Patterdale, made famous by Wordsworth, is the largest settlement, Hartsop village today being a mere hamlet increasingly taken over by part-time residents.

For many people, any mention of the Lake District triggers a memory of the verse of William Wordsworth and the inevitable 'host of golden daffodils' which were in fact seen on the shore of Ullswater. His imagery permeates our consciousness of this part of England. Interwoven with Wordsworth's romantic descriptions, there is an understanding of the relationship of man's work and the landscape in which he lived, and in part helped create. This is well expressed in his vision of the shepherd Michael:

> And grossly that man errs, who should suppose
> That the green Valleys, and the Streams and Rocks
> Were things indifferent to the Shepherd's thoughts.
> Fields, where with cheerful spirits he had breath'd
> The common air; the hills, which he so oft
> Had climb'd with vigorous steps; which had impress'd
> So many incidents upon his mind
> Of hardship, skill or courage, joy or fear;
> Which like a book preserv'd the memory
> Of the dumb animals, whom he had sav'd,
> Had fed or shelter'd, linking to such acts,
> So grateful in themselves, the certainty
> Of honorable gains; these fields, these hills
> Which were his living Being, even more
> Than his own Blood – what could they less? had laid
> Strong hold of his affections, were to him
> A pleasurable feeling of blind love,
> The pleasure which there is in life itself.

Upland farming has persisted in the Hartsop valley for centuries. Progressively, the original dense forest cover was cleared by generations of farmers. The Romans largely kept to the top of the fells, their legions making use of the High Street, a military pathway to their garrisons in the north at Hadrian's Wall. Viking invasions also left their mark on the area; experts can still identify Norse influences in the dialect and customs of the locality. Incursions by the Scots were not infrequent and noble families had occasional need to repel the northern predators. Indeed, forest clearance over and above the needs for farming was encouraged in order to deprive Scottish brigands of cover during their forays south.

In modern times, the essentially open appearance of the landscape is due to sheep rearing. Traditionally this revolved around the Herdwick sheep, an

Brothers Water – a nineteenth-century view of the Hartsop countryside

extremely hardy local breed, still favoured by the High Fell farmers. On the lower and 'softer fells' where the climate is less severe the Swaledale is a popular breed and the Cheviot strain is seen in the many cross-bred variations.

Farming activities were supplemented, when economic circumstances were favourable, by mining and quarrying. Lead has been sought in the area since Roman times and the last lead mine closed shortly before the Second World War.

The Greenside mines at Glenridding employed three hundred men in 1848 and were considered to be among the richest mines in the kingdom. Blue slates were found on the side of Place Fell, while a much-prized grey-green slate was worked for over two hundred years at Caudale Moor. A life-long resident of Hartsop, a Miss Spence of Cherry Garth, wrote an account of *Patterdale Past and Present* in 1933. In this work she mentions the Caudale Moor quarries being reopened in 1932: 'I was told recently there had been a very big order from Ireland which they could not execute as the two men sledding the slates down from the quarry could only bring eight tons a day.'[11]

On the ground, one can appreciate the enormity of such a task. The quarrymen would load something like a quarter of a ton of slate on to a long-handled wooden sledge and then run down the precipitous fell, 427 metres (1400 feet) to the valley below, braking the sledge behind them with unassisted muscle. This is one example of the prodigious labour effort that

In the centre of the picture, the zigzag sled grooves still mark the side of Caudale Moor – thousands of tons of slate were manhandled to the valley floor by this means

went into earning a living in Hartsop, which also was to leave a mark on the landscape; the tracks the sledging operations gouged in the fellside are still plainly visible on the side of Caudale Moor.

The landscape we see in Hartsop today owes a lot to the farmers of the past century – in particular the extensive dry-stone walling which is such a dominant feature of this valley, and many other upland areas of England. These walls represent further evidence of prodigious work.

As the enclosure of fellside progressed, the 'allotments' or enclosed land moved steadily up from the traditionally walled 'in bye' land which lay usually on the valley floor and closest to farms and settlements. The allotment walls were usually constructed by specialist contract labour who during the summer months would work most daylight hours. A good waller would be expected to build nine yards a day, which included gathering his own stone. The construction of a dry-stone wall is a finely developed craft and its sturdiness is witnessed by its amazing durability. Some of the gradients on which these walls were built defies the modern imagination. They are the most tangible expression of a landscape we have inherited, whose creation rested on a degree of labour availability quite different to that of today. The condition of the walls acted as indicators of the fortunes of farming at certain times, as did the extent of bracken on the hillsides which increased or decreased according to the number of sheep run on the fells.

Together with hogg houses, stone-built shelters for the hoggs or young sheep which were much used at lambing time, the residual walls represent greatly admired features of the landscape. The increasing decay of such features was partly the reason for a study of the Hartsop landscape by the Countryside Commission of England and Wales.[12] The walls had been traditionally maintained by the local farmers who, with changing economics and lack of affordable labour, now found themselves less and less able to undertake the task. Once again, the walls and other buildings have become indicators of the state of the upland economy and the general welfare of the environment.

A traditional 'hogg house' – with its clump of trees – provided shelter for the young sheep, or 'hoggs' as they are locally known

A landscape of sheer hard labour – dry-stone walling over the Fells of Cumbria remains as evidence of bygone craftsmanship

The Countryside Commission was concerned to 'identify those features which make the greatest contribution to the landscape on a macro and micro scale'. To estimate the threat to the valued landscape that contemporary circumstances posed there would also clearly need to be 'an understanding of past changes in the appearance of the landscape'. This knowledge was sought in order to allow for the 'conservation and enhancement of a valued landscape'. But what characterises a 'valued landscape' and should or indeed can one conserve or enhance it?

Changes in the landscape have always occurred whenever the economics of activities have altered. Today the economics of upland farming give rise to very different equations to the last century. Increasingly, public subsidies in the UK, as in the rest of Europe, maintain a livelihood for the hill farmers, and help to maintain a distinctive landscape for public enjoyment.

The economics of hill farming have been looked at closely and most commentators have pointed out that rearing sheep and cattle in such environmentally inhospitable areas cannot possibly compete with similar activities under more favourable conditions elsewhere in the country. In the sheltered lowlands of England and Wales, lambs appear soon after Christmas, while in the high fells of Cumbria it is often Whitsun before the hill farmers feel conditions will be suitable.

Thus farming in such areas is only viable because of the subsidies and special grants which attempt to support the more disadvantaged farmers. In receiving these subsidies, the hill farmer must acknowledge that society is underpinning his farming activities, and, as a consequence, should pay some regard to the wider usage of the hills, largely for recreation, which society increasingly demands.

The problem is one of confusion of purpose and finance. The farmer receives payment only for his farming activities through the Ministry of Agriculture. His role as a 'steward' of the upland countryside is an incidental and secondary aspect of his work. Some would argue that farmers should receive further financial help if they welcomed recreation, or actively promoted the maintenance of landscape features. In this way, more farmers could be encouraged to see the wider view of the value of the upland countryside which so many people consider a precious landscape.

Whichever way we choose to look at the present situation it raises the prospect of society altering the economics of landscape in order to avoid 'the spoiling of a precious landscape'.

But what precisely are we defining as precious and to whom? John Allen's family has farmed at Hartsop Hall for several generations. His farm amounts

A spinning gallery in Hartsop village – many of its cottages are listed of special architectural interest. They are increasingly bought for use as retirement homes or holiday properties

Hartsop Hall, beneath the snowy tops of Dove Crag. Facing north, it is 'hard' fell –
no easy place to make a living

John Allen's flock of Swaledale ewes as lambing time approaches. Many of the hill farmers are proudly independent and the necessity to supplement incomes from tourism is often resented

to some 1200 hectares (about 3000 acres), half of which lie above 1500 feet. It is almost all inhospitable north-facing land and therefore considered 'hard' fell. It supports 1300 breeding ewes. Each year, John Allen reckons some 100,000 people pass through his land, many on foot, to climb Helvellyn. The farm is owned by the National Trust.

As a farmer, John Allen receives the same headage payments for his sheep as other upland farms on lower land which can carry greater numbers of sheep. He needs to accommodate in some degree the access requirements of thousands of visitors while his landlord, the National Trust, is an organisation committed constitutionally to the preservation of parts of our landscape heritage – *for all time!*

The National Trust owns some twenty-five per cent of the Lake District. A lot of the land has been bequeathed by people who loved the landscape and wished it to be preserved forever. So at the stroke of a pen, parts of the countryside were consigned to preservation in aspic – what is preserved is often in no sense a natural landscape as we saw in the preceding chapter, but a landscape arrested at a certain stage in its evolution.

Inevitably, economic changes may require changes in the landscape which can no longer sustain certain cherished features. Who will now pay the costs of preserving these features? If the economics of hill farming do not allow the local farmers to maintain the distinctive traditional landscape, then presumably, the burden must be borne elsewhere, but what exactly are we bent on preserving and for whom? Perhaps the tourists who visit the region would be in the best position to judge what are the features in the landscape most worthy of conservation and enhancement.

It is estimated that each year at least $2\frac{1}{2}$ million people take a holiday in Cumbria and research was undertaken to discover what people saw as the principal attractions of the Lake District. The figures tabled below show, not surprisingly, a high appreciation of 'scenery', with only eleven per cent appreciation of lakes and seven per cent mountains and hills! This seems to provide further evidence that many of our ideas about landscape are conditioned as much by what descriptions we have read about a particular part of the countryside, as our own first-hand experience of it.

Survey of the main attractions of the Lake District

Type of attraction	%
Beautiful scenery	59
Peaceful atmosphere/peace and quiet	20
Good walking	12
Countryside	11
Lakes	11
Mountains/hills	7

Sample size 7116

In any event, the data in the table would seem to offer a rather dubious basis for formulating any policy for conservation determined by public taste. In further answers, roughly half of the visitors listed walking, rambling or associated activities as their preferences. Apart from isolated battles over attempted footpath closures, the Lake District has traditionally afforded good access to the walker. This is partly because Lakeland fells do not support red grouse, the breeding and shooting of which prompted many attempts to prohibit rambling over the Peak District moors and areas of Scotland. The fight for access is graphically described in Howard Hill's book *Freedom to Roam*.[13]

These struggles should not be forgotten. Over large areas of open countryside, the access enjoyed and taken for granted by so many people today was the direct result of dedicated groups of ramblers challenging the vested interest of many landowners who resented any incursion into their rights of property. Many of the protesters were fined, beaten and even imprisoned. The movement achieved great publicity particularly over 'mass trespasses' organised for areas such as Kinder Scout in the Peak District. Its cause was espoused by the *Manchester Guardian*:

> There is something wantonly perverse and profane in a society in which the rights of property can be used to defeat the emotions in which mankind has found its chief inspiration and comfort. If ever any truth lurked in the phrase 'the rights of man' those rights should surely include the right to climb mountains and the right to dream by the sea.[14]

It is an interesting reflection on the changes in our society that this sentiment taken so much for granted today should have appeared as dangerous and radical idealism sixty years ago.

Even today, though, the legal rights of access which the 1949 National Parks Act sought to encourage bears little relation to the *de facto* rights which many people assume – the full title of the Act is indeed the National Parks and Access to the Countryside Act. The strictly legal position is very different; it is estimated that, even 'allowing for "unnecessary" deductions', mining, military ranges, forests, etc., there still remains over two million hectares (8000 square miles) of open country in England and Wales. Up to 1975 public access under part 5 of the Act has been secured to only 36,912 hectares (91,215 acres). Not even this meagre total should be considered an encouraging start.

Some observers believe the tide may be going the other way. In 1978 43 orders creating new rights of way were made in England and Wales, but in the same year 303 path closure orders were made extinguishing the public's rights over some 240 kilometres (150 miles), according to the Ramblers' Association 1980.

Tourism in the Lake District today supplements local incomes in the way mining activities did in the past. In areas of great tourist pressure, the revenue to locals is greater than that to be earned by marginal farming. Apart from isolated cases of vandalism or thoughtlessness, particularly by visiting dog owners, whose animals harass the sheep, there seems little inherent conflict between the requirements of upland farmers and the visitors. As a consequence, various 'management' attempts have been undertaken, sponsored by the Countryside Commission. This ranges from mending walls to providing path markers, stiles and access agreements. Volunteer parties are put to work on a variety of schemes all intended at tidying up and easing the relationship between farmers and holidaymakers. Although a worthy scheme, these measures reinforce the philosophy that distinctive landscapes should be preserved complete with their redundant features.

It is a philosophy that has underpinned the gift of lands to the National Trust, and yet the Trust, as the major landowner in the area, is only too well

Syke-side Campsite Hartsop, a seasonal site at first opposed by the planners.
Quotas limit the number of tents. The modern trend towards country-compatible
colours for tents does much to alleviate the visual impact on open countryside

The lure of the Lakes – Ullswater

aware of the need to bow to some of the economic pressures of its tenant farmers if they are to make a living and an agricultural population is to be sustained on its lands. The dilemma of thus being drawn in opposing directions is one which the Trust is attempting to resolve in its own new policy initiative on its upland holdings, at the same time as trying to take account in its forward thinking of the bleakest of all scenarios – one in which the present support policies for upland farmers are largely withdrawn.

What is perhaps so remarkable about Hartsop and many areas of Britain's uplands is how little they have changed. The two photographs looking over the valley from John Allen's farm were taken nearly a hundred years apart. In the context of High Fell, Cumbria, man's influence is secondary to the topography. Prosperity or depression in sheep rearing may be marked by the extent of bracken on the fells or the condition of hogg houses but Hartsop is a relatively robust landscape. Its appearance has been dependent upon the amount of labour available for farm management. It is a very different situation in the English Lowlands.

A robust landscape: these two similar views of Hartsop valley show little has changed in 100 years

Chapter 4
Cropping the Countryside

These two headlines in the spring of 1984 indicate the contemporary acrimony over the impact of modern farming on the traditional countryside, particularly of lowland England. The debate has become so polarised that any degree of consensus is difficult to establish. The consequences for the countryside are critical.

'Rape' of England's green and pleasant land

By GERALD BARTLETT

BRITAIN has lost a quarter of its hedgerows, more than 126,000 miles of them, since 1945, because of intensive farming, a House of Lords committee heard yesterday.

Also grazing la...
ponds.

Environ...
the guara...
paid und...
Common A...
to cereal...
for much...
tion."

They beli...
EEC pays...
environment...
Britain's t...
landscape w...
prairies.

At presen...
grant aid...
provement"...
age and hi...
environment...
ages farme...
denude the...
would like...
money to sa...
the landscap...
happening i...
pilot scheme...

Giving joi...
Council for...
the House o...
and Environ...
yesterday, t...
Protection of...
this was an...
tunity " to e...
lation prop...
wider dema...
made on...
national ag...
during the c...

From all...
reports of fa...
ripping out...
modate co...
draining me...
out grasslan...
lucrative cer...

Damag

The counc...
of its ame...
agricultural...
objectives b...
that the pre...
tures of ag...
changed.

'DO NOT PUSH FARMERS TOO FAR' WARNING TO CONSERVATIONISTS

By GERALD BARTLETT

LEADERS of 200,000 farmers gave a warning last night that further "mindless and naive" criticism of them by conservation groups would be counterproductive.

A spokesman for the National Farmers' Union said: "Push farmers into a corner with nowhere else to go and they will go for your throat.

"Rest assured that a significant proportion will get their tractors out and rip up perhaps a grove of orchids, meadowland and hedgerows out of sheer frustration and annoyance.

"Farmers are doing an excellent job. Successive governments have exhorted them to produce more and more food and that is what they are doing.

Over the top

"Almost to a man they are conservation-conscious and there is no—or very little—gratuitous ripping up of hedgerows or other landscape amenities. Criticism so far has perhaps alerted them to conservation, but more and there could be trouble."

NFU leaders acknowledged that "certainly there are farmers who have gone over the top and done things with the environment which are exceptionally

hedgerows and meadowland by farmers alarmed at planning problems they could face.

As well as reaching a food production self-sufficiency of 80 per cent. by using new and large sophisticated machinery, farmers had increased woodland planting from 524,000 acres to 741,000 acres between 1974 and 1983.

Evidence that farmers are more conservation-conscious is the growth of Farming Wildlife Advisory Groups.

There are now branches in 50 counties, more than six counties are in the process of appointing their own advisers (helping farmers and conservationists with money and advice), and the Gloucestershire adviser is receiving 300 requests for help a year from farmers.

Planted trees

Farmers have traditionally regarded themselves as guardians of the countryside— indeed if they were removed

public they are trying and do care.

But they draw the line at having to care for and manage any area of their land adjudged to be of special environmental or scientific interest, out of their own pockets.

Among farmers who are concerned about conserving the environment, is Mr Edward Myatt, 53, who with his son Paul, 29, has just planted 100 English Oak trees and 50 Lombardy Poplars on their 415-acre Manor Farm at Thurston, Bury St Edmunds, Suffolk.

"My immediate farming neighbours and I are among those who do care about the countryside and deplore 'prairie farming' and all that involves," said Mr Myatt. "By denying the existence of caring farmers conservation groups risk alienating all farmers here in Suffolk and elsewhere.

"We have planted trees because we live here and we care what the environment looks like to us and to the village. We, like other farmers, are keeping ponds, and meadows, letting hedgerows regenerate and even planting more."

Serious rate

Mr John Popham, director of the Suffolk Preservation Society, said: "In spite of all the effort made by those members of the farming community who are conservation conscious, loss of hedgerows and other features continues at a serious rate.

"Conservation implies the sound management of resources and that means retaining and managing the remaining features of our landscape.

"The example set by Mr Myatt is one which we hope others will follow. If he can also persuade his colleagues to

The bitterness of the debate reflects a feeling of betrayal on both sides. The conservationists claim that traditionally farmers have been the custodians of the landscape, the gardeners of the countryside, which they have now largely destroyed in the pursuit of personal gain. The farmers feel equally distressed that their strenuous efforts to increase agricultural productivity and feed a far greater proportion of the country's population from home-grown produce has been repaid by a spiteful campaign of publicity abusing farmers and all their recent activities.

In between the two factions has sat an increasingly bemused public and successive governments who, by and large, have been grateful for the farmer's efforts as a contribution to Britain's balance of trade, whilst nervously watching the growing influence of those interest groups who espouse a concern for the quality of the countryside.

There certainly have been colossal changes in the post-war period which have altered the appearance of the countryside in many shires of England and Wales. How far are the changes unprecedented and irrevocable or merely a continuation in the evolution of the British countryside which has gone on for centuries? Perhaps the only common statement which can be made is that changes have always been considered alien to the 'traditional' country way of life and to the rural heritage beloved of previous generations.

Concern today over the increasing openness of the landscape is a counterpoint, to take only one example, of the widespread concern in the early nineteenth century to an encroachment of 'enclosed' landscape, as John Clare described in *The Mores*:

Fence now meets fence in owners little bounds
Of field and meadow cage as garden grounds
In little parcels little minds to please,
With men and flocks imprisoned ill at ease.

Each generation inherits the landscape of his father's farming practices and the countryside of rural England has been a canvas which illustrates the investment of capital and labour in the countryside and the potency of technology which that investment can command. If we consider the recent changes in technology, for the moment, it is soon apparent how dramatic developments have been, and how inevitable it was that these should transform our traditional image of the rural scene.

The pre-war pattern of British agriculture is one many of us can still remember from childhood experiences. It persisted in many parts of the country until the early sixties and can still be seen in those corners of Europe where the Common Agricultural Policy is as remote as the possibility of affording, or obtaining, concentrated animal feeds, herbicides, pesticides and chemical fertilisers. In such areas farmers grow what the land will allow,

plough back organic fertilisers and accept as reward for their produce whatever price the local market will pay. It is a situation which was common in England scarcely forty years ago but in the context of modern farming it seems like an echo from the Middle Ages. It is salutary to look at the sheer pace of change in recent years.

Many hands do not necessarily make light work: the hay harvest of yesteryear. Productivity was the pace of the scythe, the pitchfork and the horse

---

Map 3 *Bourne, Lincolnshire*

The south Kesteven district of Lincolnshire shows how much the modern lowland landscape has been the result of man's technology. East of the A15 road a line of villages shows the previous safe limit of settlement before drainage of the fens. Today dykes, roads, power lines and the isolated farms provide the only map features. Car Dyke, a Roman canal to the south of Bourne, shows how long man has tried to control the water elements of this landscape. In the west, estates like that of Grimsthorpe are large enough to determine the landscape quality of this part of the countryside.

It is reckoned that the last pair of oxen were ploughing in Sussex until the outbreak of the First World War. Over most of the country the motive power of the time was provided by the horse, and the strength and pace of this worthy animal determined much of the practices of farming and the appearance of the countryside.

The landscape of classic mixed farming conjures up images of languid cows grazing contentedly under Constable skies, larks ascending from ripening fields of corn, speckled with the dazzling colours of countless corn-cockles, cornflowers and poppies, hedgerows teeming with wildlife, summer swallows skimming over shimmering streams, the whole scene nurtured by the labour of besmocked rustics whose principal pleasures were a jug of cider and a day off for the Harvest Fair.

Such a landscape was also one of quite uncompromising hardship and toil. No mains electricity, or gas, little in the way of sanitation, and for the lucky

few some piped water. Labouring hours were as long as daylight, wages were low and prospects for children very limited. For the farm owners and tenants, prices for produce were rock bottom, as few could compete with foreign imports. For many bankruptcy was imminent, and in some areas landlords chose to forgo rents altogether simply to keep people in farming and the communities on the land.

British farming even in the 1930s was chronically deprived of capital, and increasingly of labour (conditions were so bad that farm workers left if any prospect of work could be found elsewhere). Of all the sectors of a sickly economy, the prospects for agriculture were among the bleakest.

And then came the war . . .

Left : The pace of twentieth-century technological change – oxen were still ploughing in Sussex up to the 1914–18 war. *Above :* One of the beasts gets a new set of shoes. Maintenance costs were low, if somewhat hazardous!

The cheap food which brought depression to producer and consumer alike became precious beyond imagining.

Its price is now reckoned in terms of human lives—the lives of the seamen who bring it here and the lives of the soldiers who depend on the ships to keep them supplied with arms.

We were producing only 30% of our food

With the Second World War the government began a campaign to systematically overhaul British agriculture

When war was declared in 1939, British agriculture was contributing only thirty per cent of the country's food. Within months, Europe was cut off completely and traditional overseas supplies had to run the gauntlet of the U-boat blockade in the Atlantic. The situation was perilous and the government was forced to take control of agriculture and use whatever measures were necessary to expand domestic agricultural production. This change in policy from virtual neglect to total control of the farming system of this country is perhaps the greatest single factor in transforming the appearance of the British countryside we see today.

Wartime policies were continued and expanded in the post-war period and our accession to the Treaty of Rome and full membership of the EEC further strengthened the system of price guarantees and market preference which had been the basis for a prosperous post-war agriculture.

Farming was ruthlessly shaken out of its pre-war rusticity and transformed into a highly-capitalised, mechanised modern industry. With guaranteed prices if they kept to quotas, farmers were additionally given a

Right : The war against Hitler won, British farmers turned to the enemy within – nature

whole range of incentives to buy new equipment, reclaim marginal land and maximise yields of all kinds of produce. As their profitability rose, farmland itself became a very attractive investment. In stark contrast to the pre-war situation, institutions – notably insurance companies – invested pension funds in land holdings.

British farmers are now but a part in a whole series of industries loosely characterised as 'agribusiness'. These have benefited from government support of agriculture every bit as much as the farmers themselves. Agricultural machinery, drainage equipment, chemical sprays, fertilisers and a galaxy of associated service industries from banking to brokering compete for business in the farming market.

Competition among these industries is now intense. In one sector of the market, tractors, for instance, there are currently thirty-four manufacturers selling to the UK market, each with perhaps six or seven different models in their range. So a significant part of UK manufacturing industry is tied up in the profitability of modern farming.

As a result of their policies, successive governments have developed a highly-organised, intensive agricultural industry capable of responding with extreme sensitivity to changes in guaranteed prices and other quota systems which are now, as a further complication, no longer decided in Whitehall but within the vastly wider context of the European Economic Community. Technology, both mechanical and chemical, is available to wreak whatever changes in production are required. The exclusion of agriculture from many planning controls has further permitted changes on a scale unimaginable before the war.

Lowland farming has become a most attractive financial proposition. A satisfactory return on capital, guaranteed by the government, tax concessions and all the other services largely supplied by the taxpayer – advisory, technical, etc. – have further strengthened the economic position of large-scale farming enterprises. The investment in terms of price support and subsidies has been a colossal one – and it is tempting to speculate what a similar investment policy in modernising our manufacturing industry may have resulted in.

The situation has not been arrived at without producing many casualties, most crucially in the sphere of wildlife conservation and in the loss of variety of landscape features. Evidence given in 1984 by the Council for the Protection of Rural England to an environment subcommittee of the House of Lords attempted to quantify the alleged losses.

They estimated ninety-five per cent of lowland herb-rich meadows had been destroyed, leaving only three per cent undamaged – this largely as a result of agricultural intensification. Eighty per cent of traditional limestone and chalk grassland had been destroyed, largely through ploughing up for arable crops or through grassland improvement with herbicides and fertilisers. Half of the lowland heaths had gone. Native broad-leaved woodland had been steadily felled with an estimated loss of ancient woodland of some thirty to fifty per cent.

It is unparalleled that such changes could have been wrought in the space of scarcely a generation. The 'timeless' appearance of the traditional countryside is now something we certainly cannot take for granted.

These changes have not affected all parts of the lowlands equally. The brunt of them has been borne largely in the traditional cereal-growing areas of East Anglia and the eastern and southern Midlands. Parts of Suffolk have received great attention with charges that their present-day appearance is more akin to the prairies of Canada than Olde England, and nowhere is this type of landscape more evident than in the Fens of Cambridgeshire and Lincolnshire.

In the western shires, where stock-rearing is more in evidence, the landscape still looks much more like the traditional English chequerboard. But the fear is that landscape change will spread inexorably from the east as the economics of large-scale farming become more and more dominant.

The most significant attempt at alleviating the landscape changes caused by today's lowland farming practices has been undertaken by the Country-side Commission. Lacking any statutory powers to intervene, the Commission launched a long campaign of persuasion. It attempted to persuade farmers that modern efficient farming did not necessarily mean they had to tear up *all* the features of the countryside. Demonstration farms were pin-pointed in key areas of the countryside where sympathetic farmers were encouraged to conserve wildlife habitats and landscape features as examples to others.

The Commission's new agricultural landscape project attempted to measure the rate of landscape change in selected areas of the lowlands. Its concern about possible changes stemmed from its belief that 'many features of the rural landscape, such as copses, hedges and ponds, no longer fulfilled a necessary function in the modern farming system. Yet it was these features which contributed so greatly to what was held to be the traditional English lowland landscape, and which provided valuable habitat and supported a variety of flora and fauna.'

The Commission's surveys found that a continuation of the *laissez-faire* attitude would not provide 'an acceptable degree of conservation of the lowland landscape'. A number of objectives were considered important. The unnecessary clearance of landscape features should be stopped and reversed by the process of planting trees and shrubs. This planting should be undertaken with financial help and advice and a good example should be set by all those managing publicly-owned land.

Combining a record harvest in Lincolnshire. British farmers in 1984 produced 26 million tonnes of cereals, 10 million more than the country can eat. Haconby Fen, Lincolnshire

Western shires still show the familiar chequerboard countryside of mixed farming. A view from Brown Clee Hill, Shropshire

The new agricultural landscape of the English lowlands – 'a *laissez-faire* response will not produce an acceptable level of conservation', claims the Countryside Commission. Near Bourne, Lincolnshire

Even in the Cotswolds the traditional pastoral scene is being threatened in many parishes, as sheep give way to the plough

The Commission also sought to encourage the interest of the media and educational authorities in the landscape. But like so many organisations attempting compromise and conciliation the Countryside Commission has suffered from detractors on both sides of the polarised groups, farmers and conservationists. The farmers have viewed with suspicion the interference of this government body as the possible first step in an orchestrated campaign to subject farmers to comprehensive controls which would make their lives increasingly more difficult and their incomes more doubtful. The conservationists, on the other hand, have scoffed at the toothless nibbling of the Commission at the urgent problem of landscape protection and have seen it only as a feeble appeasement to the farming lobby.

Even within government, the Commission has been in a difficult position. Its obvious statutory influence is through the Department of the Environment, but this department has in recent years exercised little political clout on countryside issues compared with the influence of the Ministry of Agriculture, Fisheries and Food and that most powerful of pressure groups, the National Farmers' Union.

It is interesting to note that in its latest 1984 policy statement, the Countryside Commission believes that unless there is a significant change in attitudes nationally among the farming community and within the Ministry of Agriculture, conservation policies will require statutory support.

The Commission pledges itself to another five years of persuasion and if this policy then fails planning controls will be sought. One wonders how long that might take and what would be left to protect? Yet in the mid-eighties it is possible to detect other straws in the wind; public concern is increasing over a wide range of issues and, with the hardening of attitudes to the production of agricultural surpluses at home and in the EEC, farmers themselves are beginning to see 'the writing on the wall' as the *Farmers Weekly* put it in April 1984.

The harvest of 1984 in Britain alone resulted in farmers producing a record twenty-six million tonnes of cereal grains – ten million tonnes more than the nation will consume. Given that this surplus is only realisable with taxpayers' money paid to the farmers, and further costs are incurred to keep the grain in storage, small wonder many people are questioning the continuation of policies which sprang from a wartime emergency.

To return to the headlines at the beginning of this chapter, the acrimonious debate on farming practice has been fuelled by other concerns, from straw burning to the pollution of rivers by the run-off from agricultural fertilisers. Few of Britain's water authorities can comply with current EEC standards on the amount of nitrates found in our water courses and drinking water. Other agencies are concerned about the build-up of toxins in the soil and in foodstuffs resulting from the use of herbicide and insecticide sprays.

The farming community itself contains an important lobby group of organic farmers who believe passionately in farming with nature rather than against it. It may well be that consumer reaction to certain methods of food production will lead to a shift in farming methods by the most effective means known in our society – selective market preference.

'Real ale' has been followed by campaigns for 'real bread' and 'real food'. Free-range eggs fetch a premium price which many now seem prepared to pay. Campaigns are in progress to change the emphasis on concentrated animal feeds and restore the more traditional pattern of husbandry. How far these will make any real impact on farming methods and thereby the landscape of lowland farming, it is difficult to predict.

What is more certain is the decreasing support that there now is for the concept of self-regulation by farmers in an attempt to maintain the notion – long held by the NFU – of farmers as the custodians of the countryside. The persuasive efforts of the Countryside Commission to encourage farmers in the maintenance of a diverse and interesting environment are increasingly seen, even by the Commission itself, as little more than cosmetic, whilst the local Farming and Wildlife Agricultural Groups set up in 1969, as a consortium of conservationists and farmers and aimed at bringing to the latter the expertise and know-how of conservation, appears to be largely a public relations exercise though *some* modest achievements cannot be denied. Even the 1981 Wildlife and Countryside Act is now seen by some of its original supporters to be an ineffectual instrument in the protection of some of the most important habitats against agricultural development, a matter to which we will return later. But as the arguments about the most effective form of controls which might be imposed on farmers in order to protect the landscape are pursued amongst the conservationist lobby, it does seem increasingly clear that the ever-escalating support costs for the production of food already in surplus may be a decisive factor. With grants and subsidies accounting for over eighty per cent of EEC expenditure, it has already set about reducing its outgoings to dairy farmers. If such an approach is extended to other commodities it may become less profitable in the longer term for farmers to maximise their output at the expense of the environment.

Chapter 5
Spoiling the View

FEW counties of England weave such a powerful appeal on the popular imagination as Cornwall. Its attractiveness as a holiday destination proves durable from year to year, certainly because of its beautiful scenery but also, one suspects, in its intangible 'foreignness' and mystical traditions. Its separateness from the rest of England is fostered by the Cornish themselves to whom England proper begins east of the Tamar

Now a favourite holiday haunt, this village like so many around the coast of Cornwall was part of its industrial landscape. The flourishing fishing and fish-processing industry helped support the community at Mousehole

***Map 4** St Austell*
The colossal reworking of the landscape resulting from china clay extraction is very apparent on this map. Pits have become so large that several have coalesced into giant excavations surrounded by ever-growing spoil heaps. The buoyant demand for china clay seems certain to lead to even greater expansion in the workings.

Based upon the 1984 Ordnance Survey 1:50,000 map with the permission of the Controller of Her Majesty's Stationery Office, Crown copyright reserved.

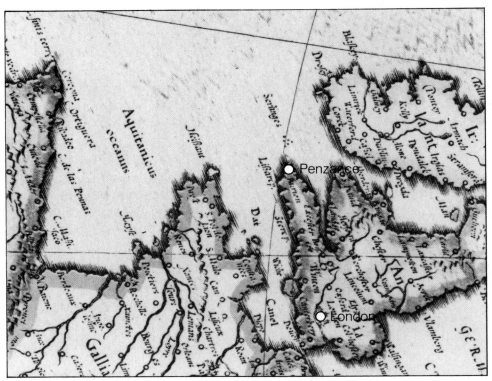

The Celtic Sea. This was not a barrier but a means of communication between the lands of Europe's western littoral

River. Centuries of relative isolation, which were only seriously eroded with the coming of Brunel's railway in 1859, contributed to Cornwall's unique identity and character. Until the railway age seaborne traffic was often preferred. Travel by sea in the eighteenth century could be quicker from Penzance to Spain than by road to London. Consequently, it is perhaps a mistake to view Cornwall from the east as a peripheral area – historically a more accurate understanding is perceived if we consider the Celtic seas not as a barrier but as a means of communication between the coastal lands of Cornwall, Wales, Brittany, the Iberian Peninsula and Ireland. From this perspective, south-east England seems 'peripheral', an idea that many Cornishmen would embrace to this day.

The landscape of Cornwall bears testimony to the continuity of man's efforts to survive in this often harsh environment.

Economically, Cornwall is as much sea as land, and livelihoods have come from both over the centuries. Today, despite the decline in Cornish fishing and the demise of the once flourishing pilchard industry, the sea, as an attraction for holidaymakers, is still a vital and prosperous element in the Cornish economy.

Cornwall, perhaps because of its demonstrable evidence of the past, today exerts a strong magnetism for those who wish to escape the pressures of the present whether for retirement or for 'dropping out' of modern society. It is a paradox that this popular image of an area so belies the relatively recent past and, one suspects, the traditions of the native people who are justifiably famous for their thrift, industry and technological acumen. These traditions have left an indelible mark on the landscape of Cornwall.

Scarcely any part of Britain can claim to have been totally unscathed by industrial activity of one sort or another at some time in its history. The mining and working of metal ores has a history in Britain that long predates the Roman invasion. For hundreds of years, these activities remained small and scattered, serving more to supplement other subsistence activities like farming or fishing. Not until the late eighteenth and nineteenth centuries did technology develop sufficiently to allow a vast increase in the scale of industrial exploitation, and with it the potential to change this landscape greatly.

It is hard to think now that in the middle of the last century large parts of Cornwall had a landscape which was arguably one of the most intensively industrialised to be found anywhere in the world. As A. C. Todd and P. Laws have observed:

> For almost two hundred years [Cornwall] was one of the most important metal mining areas in the world and the setting for tremendous enterprises in the world of engineering, its blue skies shrouded by the smoke of a thousand chimney stacks and its wildlife in the fields, moors and lanes disturbed by the roar and clatter of machines.[15]

The contemporary picture of Dolcoath (page 78) graphically illustrates the effect on the landscape the mining activities had.

The impact of the mining activities on the communities of Cornwall can be judged from this account which crops up in Friedrich Engels' classic work *The Conditions of the English Working Class*:

> In the Cornish mines about 19,000 men and 11,,000 women and children are employed in part above and in part below ground. Within the mines below ground, men and boys above twelve years old, are employed. The conditions of these workers it seems, according to the Children's Employment Commission's Report, appear to be comparatively endurable, . . . the English often enough boast of their strong, bold miners, who follow the veins of mineral below the bottom of the very sea.[16]

The above-mentioned commission had a more sobering picture of the health of the mineworkers, however:

The combination of the noxious atmosphere in the mines, high temperatures, fumes and blasting powder, together with the physical hardship of climbing up and down the mineshaft ladders, led to a much reduced life-expectancy. Most miners were exhausted and unfit for work by their mid- to late thirties, after twenty years of toil underground.[17]

Towards the end of the nineteenth century, the mining industry in Cornwall went into serious decline and barely had the smoke pall cleared over the Cornish countryside, than attitudes to the industrial past began to change.

Today, vestiges of mining activity remain striking features of the landscape; they are cherished as part of Cornwall's heritage. To many these have become objects of veneration on a par with the legendary cromlechs, and other ancient antiquities. Industrial activity in Cornwall is of interest, because it not only illustrates the ever-increasing power of applied technology to transform landscape, but it also provides a framework for us to assess how such changes affect our attitudes to landscape.

It is as well we are aware of these attitudes because they can often surface as surprisingly strong emotions: emotions which sometimes act as the mainspring for demands for intervention in industrial activities which we consider damaging to the environment, even though these activities may provide the only livelihood for local communities.

Dolcoath – a hundred years ago Cornwall had one of the most industrialised landscapes in the world

The wreck of the *Cromdale*, a three-master that broke up in two hours, pounded by a sou'westerly gale

Before large-scale metal workings, much of Cornwall had a meagre economy of poor farming, supplemented with fishing. Traditionally, the local population would have had recourse to the more romantic, if hazardous, activities of smuggling. The wild coastline and frequent storms could bring other bounty such as booty from shipwrecks. Such incidents were not infrequent but they serve to emphasise the almost daily hardships and hazards which Cornish families endured in winning a livelihood. Mining, whenever the metal price was adequate, provided another source, and again a dangerous one, of securing income.

One of the most spectacular landscapes of industrial Cornwall, even today, is that around St Just in West Penwith. Here two major mine complexes at Botallack and Levant still dramatically evoke the economic landscape of the past. The Harvey beam engine at Levant Mine is now preserved by the National Trust. It is one example of the type, and many were much larger, which enabled the large-scale underground mining operations. In the case of the coastal workings at Botallack and Levant they allowed mining to be undertaken far out, under the bed of the sea. This particular engine has an

'The Crowns' at Botallack, 'a combination of the powers of art with the wild sublimity of nature'

added significance as it is also the very first to be preserved in Cornwall. It marks, in 1935, the birth of the industrial conservation movement and is thus the local pioneer of the ever-increasing popular interest in industrial archaeology.

Even in its heyday, the industrial activities of Botallack provoked ambivalent reactions from contemporary commentators:

> . . . But if you are thus struck and surprised at the scene when viewed from the cliff above, how much greater will be your wonder if you descend to the surface of the mine. You will then behold a combination of the powers of art with the wild sublimity of nature which is quite unparalleled.[18]

It is interesting to see that the activities here were encompassed in the word 'art' in that description. Others, though, were less taken with the appearance of the landscape:

... Descending the valley [at Levant] we climb the opposite hill, past mud and miners, arsenic fumes and tramlines, till we reach the top. But the face of the land is still marred and rendered hideous by mining operations. The path winds bravely westwards but no longer through flowers and ferns, but over a stunted and blasted heath, denuded of vegetation with unsightly refuse heaps of rock and clay.[19]

Also of Cape Cornwall:

... across the cove is Cape Cornwall, another lofty peninsula stretching far into the sea ... Alas, its very apex is crowned with a chimney stack, and the water in the cove is discoloured by mining operations. Let us hurry on, though man does mark the earth with ruin, we need not linger in it. *ibid*

At Levant and Botallack we can still trace clearly the functional relationship of the mining operations and their impact on the landscape. The workings in this area yielded at varying times not only the traditional tin and copper but also arsenic and other minerals.

What clearing the arsenic from flues would have been like in its heyday

Looking at these ruins today, one imagines few would advocate their destruction and removal, yet are our perceptions and feelings merely coloured by nostalgia? How far could one consider the relationship between industry and landscape an art form? In their book *The Industrial Archaeology of Cornwall*, Todd and Laws claim:

> ... the industrial archaeologist has an important contribution to make to what may be defined as the aesthetics of industry; engine houses that take on the appearance of Cornish chapels; granite stairways in mines that are as beautifully designed as any in a church tower; factories that were made to look like the coach houses of the gentry; chimney stacks that for their mathematical precision of construction bear comparison with the columns of a Roman temple, and crushing mills that one could easily mistake for part of a medieval monastery.

An engine house against the sunset – a much-loved cliché of the Cornish countryside
Left: Remains of the old arsenic flues at Botallack, Cornwall

But is this an attitude we can only apply to the past? Certainly the noise and strife have gone, the terrible fumes from the arsenic works have gone, and the scars of wasteland have been overgrown. But how far is it possible today to consider working industrial landscapes as 'art', as J. A. Paris did in the early 1800s?

Contemporary attitudes to industrial landscapes have often been characterised by an incensed outrage at the legacy of industrial dereliction, as John Barr has written:

> Dead or still growing the [spoil] heaps are monuments to man's degrading presence. And it is not only the dirt dumps, man's lust for coal, clay for pottery, clay for bricks, limestone and sand, sandstone and slate and chalk and gravel for building houses, building roads, all the extractive industries essential for national prosperity, yet which gouge and tear the earth ... Man's ingenuity turned to ways of ripping his landscape apart ...
>
> This dereliction kills vast acres of a small nation; at its ugliest it kills the spirit of the people who live amidst it.[20]

The same author goes on to claim:

> The county with the greatest dereliction, just over 6500 hectares (around 16,000 acres), was not in the old industrial north but Cornwall, principally the result of china clay workings. *ibid*

The reaction to china clay workings has often been extremely hostile. The industry itself has been in a dilemma. To work the clay economically, ever bigger and deeper pits need to be excavated. The kaolin tends to get purer and more valuable with depth and many pits have no known 'bottom', other than that imposed by the technology of excavation and the economics of waste disposal. Waste quartz sand constitutes seven times the volume of the clay gleaned and unlike other quarrying operations cannot be back-filled into the existing hole, for fear of covering the very deposits being mined.

Demand for the product, which has a myriad of uses from paper fillers to pharmaceuticals, continues to grow and there is little doubt the industry makes a major contribution to the national economy and a dominant one in the earnings of many Cornish people.

Today, the effect of the workings on the landscape around St Austell and Bodmin is extremely visible; attitudes towards this part of Cornwall's countryside could not be more polarised. Paradoxically, it is mainly writers and poets, like Jack Clemo, who have found virtue in this landscape:

> Odd coincidence that Wesley and Cookworthy invaded Cornwall at almost the same time ... both started processes which changed the material landscape. Gaunt little Methodist chapels sprang up like

mushrooms in nearly every village and the whole hill country between
St Austell and Goss Moor became scarred by small white excavations,
which gradually deepened and widened with more and more buildings
at the pit heads until they grew into the massive china clay industry as
we know today, pulsing with electrical equipment and yet retaining its
original crude menace as a volcanic and seismic disturbance.[21]

The most famous champion of traditional china clay scenery is the writer
Daphne du Maurier:

... In the china clay country is the strange, almost fantastic beauty of
the landscape, where spoil heaps of waste matter shaped like pyramids
point to the sky, great quarries formed about their base descending into
pits filled with water, icy green like arctic pools.
   ... These clay heaps with their attendant lakes and disused quarries
have the same grandeur as tin mines in decay but in a wilder and more
magical sense.[22]

The penchant of the Cornish and their admirers to indulge in Celtic
mysticism is another legend of the landscape in these parts, but magical or
no, other profound emotions have been stirred by these spoil heaps. The
poet, Jack Clemo, a Cornishman himself, uses sexual imagery:

You never saw
The clay as I have seen it, high
On the bare hills, the little breasts
So white in the sun, all the veins running white
Down to the broad womb with its scars.[23]

Other writers have had other emotions stirred by the 'lunar landscape'. The
white conical tips have been described as 'pustules on a leprous landscape'.
This kind of reaction has been popular in recent times, exemplified in a
description of a bus-ride from Bodmin to St Austell, taken by Peggy Pollard:

... passing through the white leprous country with the pyramidal
pustules of spoil heaps, the unnatural jade green pools at their feet –
some call them beautiful. For myself I am only impatient of the
slowness of gorse and heather to hide them. The soil is loaded with
arsenic and scarcely anything can grow but only heath, brooms and
furze.[24]

Public outcry eventually caused the major company in the area, English
China Clays, to attempt a 'landscaping' of their spoil heaps. One example of
the results can be seen on Hensbarrow.
   Considerable research has been undertaken to find grasses which will
successfully colonise the almost sterile quartz sand spoil heaps. The work has

involved great expense and there is no doubt it has ameliorated the local nuisance of dust pollution in the atmosphere. This attempted 'restoration' of the landscape brings us back to an underlying question of aesthetics. At best, the levelled-off tips provide a meagre pasture on features which are clearly not part of the original topography. Du Maurier clearly thinks they should have left well alone and the industry should have allowed nature to recolonise the wastelands:

> . . . Wild flowers struggle across the waste, seeds flourish into nameless plants, wandering birds from the moorland skim the lakes or dabble at the water's edge. Seagulls flying inland hover above the surface. There is nothing ugly here. Cornishmen are wresting a living from the granite as they have done through countless generations, leaving nature to deal in her own fashion with forgotten ground which being prodigal of hand, she has done with a lavish and careless grace.

China clay spoil heaps near St Austell – one of Britain's most extensive mining landscapes. Nowadays many are levelled and vegetated
Right : '. . . the strange, almost fantastic beauty . . . the same grandeur as tin mines in decay but in a wilder and more *magical* sense'

The key sentiment here must be the economic – 'Cornishmen wresting a living from the granite' – and perhaps we should confront the modern workings of the industry at their most extreme. In the huge china clay pits we see exactly what china clay workings mean to the landscape. Is this a landscape that needs always to be ignored, fenced off and if possible concealed from public gaze, or does it possess some intrinsic interest and could it ever be considered even a beautiful landscape?

In the United States, gigantic excavations are often part of the tourist itinerary. The open-pit mining at Bingham Canyon in Utah is just one example. For such a small country, Britain, thanks to its geological diversity, has a great number of mineral excavations.

If the old slate workings in Snowdonia have been commercialised to form quite an important tourist attraction, along with some of the tin mines of West Cornwall, could not the same be done for the huge limestone quarries of the Pennines or the chalk pits of southern England, or must a patina of age, if not romance, be added before this becomes possible? If the sheer size of excavations adds a vital awe-inspiring element in North America – something we in Britain cannot hope to emulate – perhaps it is the association of the popular *Poldark* novels of Winston Graham with the Cornish tin mines that has provided the appreciative key.

But perhaps the real paradox is that the disused quarries and the remnants of old industrial workings now provide inviting habitats for many plants and animals ousted from their more traditional rural haunts – often by modern farming methods. Indeed the Nature Conservancy Council has gone so far as to stress the importance of such areas.

Chapter 6
Rural Retreat

SO far in this book we have concentrated on various aspects of rural change in the open countryside, but the villages and hamlets scattered across the landscape of England and Wales are just as much a part of the countryside and also have a story of change to tell. The agricultural revolution has been, in part, generated by demands for increased food production from the towns, and many of the changes within the villages have an urban origin, too. But before this and over a prolonged period change in the village was commonly characterised by the inexorable process of population loss.

These losses had their beginnings at a time when most villages were largely based upon agriculture and began in earnest when new farming technology started to make its mark in the nineteenth century. The rural riots and rick-burning of the 1830s and 1840s were, for example, the result of unemployment brought about by the introduction of reapers and binders replacing the old labour-intensive methods of harvesting with the scythe. As the new mechanised techniques swept across the country diminishing the need for labour, the towns were increasingly seen as not only offering higher wages, but a better and fuller way of life. The flight from the land was increased in this century by the agricultural depression of the years between the two World Wars and then further reinforced by a boom in agriculture after 1945 that demanded greater capital and smaller labour forces than ever before to achieve ever-rising levels of productivity.

By the 1960s, agricultural employment had declined to such an extent that, from being the largest occupational group in England and Wales in 1815, it had become the smallest. The prosperity of a capital-intensive agriculture was endorsed by post-war legislation in the form of price support for key commodities and capital grants for a whole range of farm improvements, but the use of planning controls under the Town and Country Planning Act of 1947 to protect the appearance of rural areas meant that the villages could offer little by way of alternative employment. The building of new factories and warehouses was largely discouraged outside towns, and other post-war legislation, aimed at the redistribution of industry throughout Britain, helped to see to it that such industrial development was kept well away from the countryside.

The overall improvements in transport and standards of living did bring some new jobs to the rural areas through the development of tourism and its

related services, but their impact, being geared more often than not to seasonal part-time female employment, was at most marginal. The migration to the towns and centres of employment brought in its wake further reductions in local opportunities. As people moved away, so the demand for services declined. Shops, pubs, garages and other facilities were shut down, so making the towns even more attractive.

Yet, by the 1960s, a counterflow began to be marked in some areas, with people moving out from the towns to the villages to reoccupy the now-empty cottages and convert and name as houses buildings that were once occupied by those lately defunct local services. House names such as 'the old school', 'the old forge', 'the old bakehouse', 'the old mill-house', showed what the

Leafy Sussex shades the village of Ditchling from the high summer sun

Map 5 *Ditchling and the Downs*
The main railway lines to London run like arteries through the commuter countryside of Sussex. The Downs, still fortunately undeveloped, look down on the steadily expanding settlements. How long before Burgess Hill merges with Hassocks, Keymer and Ditchling?

Based upon the 1984 Ordnance Survey 1:50,000 map with the permission of the Controller of Her Majesty's Stationery Office, Crown copyright reserved.

village had once supported. The newcomers, plus those who were left of the original community, relied largely on private transport to reach services based in the towns. If they were not amongst the affluent retired, the newcomers not only worked in urban centres, commuting to these from their new village homes, but could *afford* to remain dependent on their own means of getting to the towns to fulfil even their most basic needs.

People such as these, in turn, forced others to leave the villages by increasing the price of housing and competing in the market for the most desirable period residences. Most of these newcomers had been attracted by the image of the village as a pleasant and desirable place to live in, not only because of its physical attributes and its greater availability of living space – certainly by comparison with a town or even a suburban environment – but because of a belief that friendliness, co-operation and community spirit remain the attributes of all who live in villages. It is a belief that has been long promoted in popular books about the countryside and more recently by radio and television.

One of the contributors to *The Shell Book of English Villages*[25] was even prompted to write that 'more than Big Ben or Westminster Abbey, the English village is the visual symbol of our way of life'. That television commercials for wholemeal bread, breakfast cereals, even the Royal Mail, have intensified the countryside's appeal by the careful use of special camera filters to prettify the local scene is no accident; it is the well-researched foundation on which an effective sales campaign may be maintained. Whatever the reality and however illusory, undoubtedly the image of the village remains for many suffused by a roseate view of the values of its life. Drawn to the village by such distorted images, the newcomers, perhaps surprisingly, have merely helped to reinforce the popular image of the community at least in so far as its outward appearances are concerned. Through their hanging flower baskets, their manicured cottage gardens, their renovated picturesque properties, their craft and antique shops, all in place of rough and simple dwellings and a main street characterised by the provision of the most basic of services, they have succeeded in helping to create the largely cosmetic rural flavour of the television advert – an attempt, perhaps, to turn myth into reality.

And this trend, in turn, has given momentum to the invasion of the more affluent.

The extent to which villages conform to this model varies to a great extent according to the nature of the village and its ownership and the degree to which it enjoys ready accessibility to nearby towns. The frequently used terminology of the 'open' and the 'closed' village is helpful here. 'Closed' villages, those where ownership of land and property is in the hands of one person or one family, will clearly be different from 'open' villages where ownership is widely spread throughout the community. Thus in the case of the village which forms the core of an extensive estate and may well house many of the estate workers, an influx of newcomers will have been avoided. An extreme example of this is Great Tew in north Oxfordshire where the estate owner has made it his deliberate policy to let whatever housing that exists in excess of estate needs *only* to those who will work in the village. Commuting is definitely out. But the 'closed' village has never been a common occurrence and, in addition, many such estates and their attendant 'closed' villages have, in this century, been broken up and sold to meet death duties. As Lady Bracknell put it in Oscar Wilde's *The Importance of Being Earnest*, 'What with the duties expected of one during one's lifetime and the duties exacted from one after one's death, land has ceased to be either a profit or a pleasure. It gives one position and prevents one from keeping it up. That's all that can be said about land.' What is evident is that most villages in England and Wales are of the 'open' type and here the extent to which newcomers represent an important new element in the village is very much a product of the accessibility of nearby towns and the desirability of the village as a place to live.

To illustrate some of these points about change in the village we need take but one example – that of Ditchling in East Sussex. A visit to one of the two house agents now apparently flourishing in the village high street soon makes it clear what the attractions of this village are to the newcomer. As a senior partner in one of the firms put it, 'First and foremost is the question of easy access to London for the commuter'.

A frequent electric train service to London's Victoria Station is available not three kilometres (two miles) distant at Hassocks, whilst eight kilometres (five miles) to the north is that archetypal commuter station, Haywards Heath. Either way, one can be in the centre of London inside an hour. Also the A23 trunk-road (now in part replicated by a motorway) offers a good alternative for rapid access to the metropolis. Ditchling is also attractive to the businessman working in Brighton some 9.5 kilometres (six miles) to the south across the South Downs. Not only is this robust seaside resort beloved of the day-tripper and conference-goer, but is now the centre of new technologically-based light industry and the ever-growing finance and insurance sectors. Given the delights of the physical surroundings of Ditchling nestling as it does beneath the Downs, the protection it enjoys from the expansion of its neighbour Keymer as a result of its own miniature green-belt, plus the aesthetic pleasures offered by the nearby Glyndebourne opera house and the more earthy charms of the adjacent Plumpton racecourse, all in addition to good accessibility, small wonder that Ditchling is residentially popular. It is also no surprise that it is impossible to purchase a house for less than £34,000 in the village. Even the very cheapest end of the

Ann of Cleves' house, Ditchling – the timelessness of English villages enhances the appeal of a country lifestyle

Ditchling from the South Downs and, beyond, the ever-sprawling villages of Sussex. *Right :* Under the South Downs, a spacious way of life has its own impact on the countryside

property market is only met from the sale of council houses on the estates located to the north and south of Ditchling.

Because of the constraints placed on the growth of the built-up area, 'in-filling' has been the popular way of increasing the housing stock. Many of the old allotments, orchards and large gardens near the heart of the village have fallen to the developer.

At the upper end of the market, the wealthiest commuters want to exercise their desire for space in a way which could not be fulfilled in or near London, by the purchase of a house plus a few acres on which perhaps to keep horses. Land for this purpose has become available around Ditchling from that store of it previously held by farmers. Research carried out by Ruth Gasson in the 1960s and Peter Corrigan in the early 1970s has clearly demonstrated the break-up since 1945 of agricultural holdings all along the major access corridor from London to Brighton which encompasses the main railway line and the A23.

A case-study of Ditchling parish, in particular, indicates not only the high degree of fractionalisation of holdings close to the village itself but that the sales of paddock-sized parcels of land have shown a strong upward trend from the mid 1950s right through the 1960s. It is perhaps not surprising to learn then that today only one full-time farmer still has land abutting the village settlement of Ditchling. Even he has succumbed to the demands of the 'horsey-culture' fraternity by converting his barns to loose-boxes. And like so many other farmers in the area he has sold off his attractive old East End Lane farmhouse, choosing to live in a small modern dwelling.

A walk along East End Lane shows admirably the wide variety of houses now occupied by the retired or the commuter. Close in, the conversion of agricultural workers' cottages is much in evidence. One passes then through the developments of this century, particularly the inter-war years, where the building is characterised by its quality and the traditional Sussex style. The warm maturity of houses here surrounded by gardens ablaze in high summer with hollyhocks and roses would grace the front of any quality chocolate-box. The occasional 'in-filling' of a modern property is apparent before the lane gives way at the periphery of the village to the larger 'houses with land'.

Nowhere in evidence is the home of the agricultural worker, the village postman or the butcher, the baker or the candlestick-maker. Fifty years ago if you had turned from East End Lane into the High Street at its northern end and walked south to the village centre, as Kelly's Trade Directory confirms, you would have found a dozen or so commercial enterprises serving the needs of the villagers. Where are they now? True, the Bull Hotel and the Sandrock Inn are still public houses; one butcher still remains as does a grocer. But the fishmonger's is now an antique shop as is one of the other grocers. The hardware store has gone; the baker's has become an electrical store and the florist's and greengrocer's has become a craft pottery shop. The present shop of a furniture restorer was once an outlet for groceries, whilst the dairy shop is now the Ditchling tea-rooms. Important personal services such as those provided by the boot repairer's and the chemist are no more and their premises converted to private houses. The two Ditchling branch banks were additions of the late 1930s to the village high street's range of services as the affluence of the community began to increase. Then rationalisation and centralisation saw their demise in the 1970s, at a time when banking was becoming less and less a matter of class. At the same time other important *public* services were eroded. At the end of the 1960s the village boasted many buses a day to Brighton and back, as well as a very frequent service throughout the day to Keymer and Hassocks, to Burgess Hill and to Haywards Heath and Lewes. Now there are only nine buses on a weekday, which make the journey to and from Hurstpierpoint and to and from Burgess Hill and these cluster around the mornings and evenings. Only two buses connect in each direction with the nearest towns of Haywards Heath and Lewes, again running in the early morning and early evening. Worst of all there is now no direct service at all to the regional shopping and service centre of Brighton.

In terms of educational provision perhaps Ditchling is less typical and has fared better than many comparable villages, for a new Church of England primary school was built and opened quite recently. This apart, the overall reduction in sales outlets and services reflects situations elsewhere in many similar villages which are in the shadow of large towns. It underlines the capacity of the affluent newcomers, now in the majority in the village and whose work is outside it, through their mobility and wealth to seek the goods and services they need elsewhere.

The problems arise for the residual population of agricultural and other lowly-paid workers, and for the elderly and the young whose access to the facilities they need may be severely curtailed. For even Ditchling has some less well-off inhabitants in the two large council estates. But in whatever way the problems that exist for certain minority sections of the community are viewed and the propensity of the newcomers to create a synthetic rural idyll considered, the presence of the latter cannot always be thought of as undesirable. As John Hadfield has written in *The Shell Book of English Villages*:

One raises an eyebrow at the pseudo-Georgian front doors, the carriage lamps, the bottle glass window panes, the poker burnt name plates, the swimming pools and the firms' cars lining the lanes. But in fact it may well be the commuter who is the saviour of the village. He has taken over and restored the tumbledown cottages vacated by the farm labourer.

First train to town – the crack-of-dawn commuter resigned to the routine travel

So far undeveloped, the heart of the village retains its green, its duckpond and its charm. Ditchling, Sussex

Top : West Street, Ditchling: past generations have left their cottages to different sorts of folk. *Above :* Village shops and services face a dubious future

The commuter may be absent all day, but in the evenings or at weekends he will attend meetings of the parish council, he will help organise the flower show, he will join the local preservation society. His wife may become president of the Women's Institute and on Sundays . . . he and she may fill the church pews where once the lord and lady of the manor sat.[25]

This quotation has more than an element of truth in it for Ditchling and other villages like it. Indeed the sentiments of the Ditchling Preservation Association's chairman cannot but be admired when he speaks of the need to maintain individual buildings of historical interest and the overall character of the centre of the village with its delightfully harmonious appearance made up from a mix of buildings that span the centuries. And although a newcomer, he recognises the importance of not pickling the village in aspic, of encouraging a community that is broad in its social and economic make-up, and of accepting change through a process of evolution rather than revolution.

Certainly such views have a wide following amongst those who look to the future, not for change of the kind that has occurred over the past twenty years, but for the realisation of better-balanced village communities. The question is how this might be achieved. In this respect it is easy to criticise policies of local government which have encouraged the centralisation of services in certain 'key villages' and not others, and the priority given in investment terms at national level to the older industrial centres to the neglect of the rural areas. Against this, however, must be set the establishment of the Development Board for Rural Wales which has responsibilities for social and economic community development. It has powers to acquire land and develop property; to encourage and sponsor industrial, commercial and other forms of development; to build local houses and to assist local authorities financially. In England a Development Commission has promoted special investment and rural development area strategies and set up the Council for Small Industries in Rural Areas (COSIRA) as a special agency to facilitate the development of rural industries in rural areas. Many of these have been of the local craft type – Ditchling's pottery enterprise is a good example. It has also attempted to increase the resources of Rural Community Councils so that they can expand their task of bringing rural issues to the attention of local and central government, as well as promoting self-help projects to offset some of the effects of change in villages. For example, it has been the spur to development of unconventional services and local facilities for the elderly such as a community-run transport service using mini-buses. Ditchling has such a scheme.

But the problem appears to be that even where rural needs are recognised and solutions proposed, the resources made available to achieve their resolution are not enough. Many would argue that the removal of schools and other services from villages must not be judged on economic but community grounds; that the construction of council houses for locals is useless unless matched by jobs and these are only likely if there is a greater willingness to permit some forms of industrial development in rural areas. It is here at least that a recent directive from the Department of the Environment to planning authorities may be seen as a move in this direction with the tight controls on such developments that have been the linchpin of rural policies over the last quarter-century now considerably relaxed. However, for the rest of these objectives to be achieved, central government would certainly need to make available levels of investment which approach those devoted of late to the regeneration of inner-city neighbourhoods.

Chapter 7
Conserving the Coast

AS we saw in the last chapter, increasing personal wealth and improvements in communications give people greater freedom of choice of where they can afford to live and still maintain their town-based incomes. It is highly likely that the revolution in information systems currently under way with data processors, video-phones, home tele-banking, etc., will further accelerate this move and, it is argued, lead to the progressive dispersal of households over a much wider area of the countryside.

Combine these factors with the increasing popularity of maritime-based recreation and it seems likely that pressures for development will intensify on one very finite part of the nation's countryside – the coast.

A time there was when pressures on the coast were somewhat less severe. The motor car was to change all that

---

Map 6 *Purbeck Heritage Coast, Dorset*
From the Sandbanks ferry across Poole harbour the Dorset Coast Path begins its route towards the south-west. It traverses a landscape of extraordinary variety and interest. Its geology and plant and animal life enhance scenery of tremendous beauty. Can this be preserved for future generations?

Today, the coast of southern England is already a testament to the popularity of coastal living. From Dover in the east to Bournemouth in the west, we see a coastline that has been almost entirely urbanised for a length of over 230 kilometres (145 miles).

There have been other major pressures on coastal developments. The technology of bulk carriers for oil, minerals and container traffic has led to large sites being built up as transhipment points for oil tankers, iron ore carriers and container ships. These sites have usually been on undeveloped coasts rather than in traditional docklands which have been largely allowed to collapse into dereliction.

The electricity-generating industry has sought coastal sites for nuclear power stations from Dungeness to Wylfa and it seems inevitable that further development of offshore oil extraction will lead to increased land needs along the coasts of the English Channel and the Irish Sea.

Concern over the state of the coastline was first expressed in the 1930s: *The English Coast : Its Development and Preservation* was a report by the Council for the Protection of Rural England (the Dougill Report), published in 1936.[26] The major concerns revolved around the growth of motor car ownership in a country where nowhere was more than 160 kilometres (100 miles) away from the coast. The report saw the problems in 1936 as being ribbon development (part of a wider concern over the expansion of towns along the main roads). This would inevitably screen the landscape and incidentally involve costly services. More specific to the coast were the eyesores of shacks, bathing huts in all manner of shape, size and colour; picnic grounds without shelter or sanitation with their attendant problems of litter; kiosks, temporary shops, refuse dumps and hoardings together with car parks; and the loss of access any development caused with the building over of footpaths and an increase in risk of coastal erosion in popular areas.

Dougill came out with surprisingly radical proposals for dealing with these problems. Nothing less than public ownership of the coast was sought to ensure outdoor recreation and preserve scenic views.

This CPRE report, of course, predated any comprehensive planning laws in Britain which were not introduced until the 1947 Town and Country Planning Act. Dougill did make specific suggestions as to guidelines which present-day planners might endorse. Buildings should be concentrated away from the coastal headlands, roads should be routed away from the coast, and open space should be protected and enhanced by tree planting and landscaping.

Thus a considerable public campaign was under way when the war broke out, but the necessity to turn Britain into a fortress had in itself an incalculable impact on the coast. Wartime military needs deprived people of access to much of the coast and led to a great deal of squalid development.

Some of the measures, such as the appropriation of a large area of the Dorset coast for the gunnery ranges at Lulworth, remain today, and everywhere one sees remnants of coastal defences littering the foreshore and cliffs.

Interest and concern after the war was soon renewed by the National Trust. The 1961 Census showed a marked increase in the number of people living in coastal districts and a report by the National Trust in 1962 was alarming. It reckoned that of the 4425 kilometres (2750 miles) of the coastline of England and Wales, some 3058 kilometres (1900 miles) was 'already beyond redemption' owing to development of one sort or another. Furthermore, the report went on, 'the remaining 1448 kilometres (900 miles)' were 'under constant development pressure and that outright ownership by the Trust was the only permanent safeguard'.

The National Trust put its faith to safeguard the coast, or what remained of it, in their unique powers granted by a 1907 Act of Parliament under which land could be held by the Trust and declared inalienable – it could only be sold, lost or appropriated through Act of Parliament, a procedure which the Trust pointed out had never been invoked despite two World Wars.

In 1965, the National Trust launched an appeal called 'Enterprise Neptune' to get funds to buy the underdeveloped coast and protect the heritage. The government of the day donated £250,000. By 1981, the National Trust had acquired a further 362 kilometres (225 miles) of coast to add to its previous 300 kilometres (187 miles). Its total holding of 663 kilometres (412 miles) was reckoned to constitute some fifty per cent of the outstanding coastline in the country remaining largely undeveloped.

In more recent time the concerns of the National Trust about the coast have been echoed by the Countryside Commission – who now finance a considerable part of National Trust conservation policies – amounting to £750,000 in 1980.

The Commission itself has sought to extend protection of the coastline by its policy of defining Heritage Coasts and instituting a package of policies which rest on promoting voluntary co-operation of local authorities, landowners, conservation groups and other interested parties in preventing further adverse development along the coastline.

The Purbeck Heritage Coast in Dorset is one such defined area. Along its length from Studland in Poole Harbour to Weymouth in the west, we can see examples of the pressures our coast is under, and the sort of policies which it is hoped can meet the challenge of preserving what some would claim is the only part of our 'natural' countryside – the coast.

Moving west along the Heritage Coast path we soon encounter a natural landscape at Shell Beach, Studland, which is the first open undeveloped stretch of coastline for over 230 kilometres (145 miles). It is owned by the National Trust, and includes the Studland nature reserve, consisting largely of sand dunes and heath. It is nationally important, being uniquely the home of all British reptile species. It is managed by the Nature Conservancy Council. Within Poole Harbour is Brownsea Island given by Baden-Powell, founder of the Scout movement, to the National Trust. Shell Beach is immensely popular and its atmosphere of getting away from it all is congenial to naturists as well as naturalists. Summer weekends find the car parks full very early in the mornings.

Further west, the chalk of southern England outcrops in the spectacular Old Harry Cliffs. Here a series of perpendicular cliffs some 100 metres high (around 328 feet), together with their distinctive stacks and arches, make up a classic example of southern England chalk coastline. The cliffs are popular nesting sites for a variety of sea birds. On the top of the cliffs, chalk downland flowers are found in profusion, where agriculture has not encroached too near the cliff edge. Extensive arable acreages are now found right up to the coast path and these present a threat to the native flora, which in places has to survive in scarcely more than the path's width.

An early attempt at popularising the coast is now seen within the grounds of what is the Durlston Country Park. Owned and run by the Dorset County Council, it contains Durlston Castle and a rather curious globe. These were the works of a Victorian eccentric who sought to make Durlston Point a globally significant point for visitor interest. The globe itself is made of Portland stone and has all manner of geographical data carved on it to help

Old Harry Rocks. The chalk cliffs eroded by the sea into arches and stacks. Here at least they remain undeveloped and uncommercialised

Portland Stone quarries at Winspit: the much-prized building stone occurs in a band, and galleries were driven into the cliff face to exploit it. These caves are now a favourite haunt of bats

the visitor orientate to the wider world. The Dorset coast, like many others in Britain, has attracted somewhat esoteric enthusiasms as witnessed by the surprising number of follies and other artefacts found in prominent locations. Modern opinion is rather ambivalent about their contribution to the coastal amenity. The Clavell Tower in Kimmeridge is one example which provokes some people to wish it an unkindly early demise.

Inland from the coast, the Isle of Purbeck possesses a tremendous heritage landscape. Part of the heartland of Thomas Hardy's Wessex, it forms an integral part of the coast's attractions. Many Purbeck towns are probably known as well by Hardy's fictitious names as their real ones – Anglebury for Wareham for example. The brooding ruins of Corfe Castle emerging from the early morning mists give a timelessness to the landscape unsurpassed anywhere.

The local Portland stone, still quarried and worked on a small scale, is one of the most harmonious building materials ever used. Villages like Kingston, Worth Matravers and Langton Matravers, as well as larger settlements such as Corfe, seem to have grown out of the country rock.

Down on the cliffs below Seacombe and Winspit, we can see the abandoned galleries where Portland stone was quarried directly from the cliff face. Another rich stone is the so-called Purbeck Marble; not a genuine marble but capable of being highly polished, this was a much-sought-after building material – much of central London is built of it. The workings today, although somewhat dangerous for human exploration, provide a refuge for a rare species of bat whose fortunes in contemporary Britain have been sadly in decline.

At St Aldhelm's Head, a fine limestone headland, is found the curious St Aldhelm's Chapel, a squat square building which from the distance looks more like a Bedouin tent than a Norman church. The building is still used as a place of worship and is one further example of the continuous settlement of this countryside which stretches back far beyond Christian times. Behind much of the coastline of this part of Dorset the steep, dry valleys leading inland have a clearly visible pattern of terraces. These are strip lynchets, believed to be past agricultural features which allowed the ploughing and cultivation of these areas in medieval times when the rural population was much greater than today.

Looking west from St Aldhelm's Head are a series of headlands. The white limestone gives way to the darker rock of Kimmeridge clay, introducing yet another important feature of this part of England.

The geological diversity of this coastline is an immense asset. Apart from the aesthetic variety it imparts to the scenery, it is a much-used teaching resource for a wide range of academic subjects. The coast during school term is often swarming with students of geology and geography. One consequence of the geological variety is a great diversity in plant species and the interest does not end at the shoreline. At Kimmeridge is established one of the country's first marine nature reserves. Supervised by the Dorset Naturalists' Trust, the hope is to foster interest in marine wildlife and ensure its survival. The very real possibility of large-scale off-shore oil extraction is one development being closely monitored in Dorset.

In the convoluted geology of the area the chalk reappears further west and provides two popular features of the landscape – Durdle Door, a natural arch, and Lulworth Cove, where the sea has broken through to etch out a perfect cove in the softer clay strata. Both of these features are 'honeypots' in the parlance of the tourist trade, and attract umpteen thousands of visitors. To many these are *the* attractions of the Dorset coast. In their very popularity lies the danger that too great a pressure of visitors could simply overwhelm the natural beauty of the sites. Both are in land owned by long-established estates who have endeavoured, with varying success, to cater for the huge demand. The very large car park in Lulworth and the caravan site at Durdle Door need continual sensitive planning provisions if they are not to spoil the appearance of the coast.

Along the length of coast from Studland to Weymouth, there are two gaps in the defined Heritage Coast. These are the seaside towns of Swanage and Weymouth. Traditional resorts, these have catered for tourists for many generations. George III popularised Weymouth, and His Majesty on horseback is cut as a chalk figure on the Downs above the town. Until the explosion in personal car ownership, the seaside town provided for many of Britain's summer holidaymakers. Seaside landladies in their boarding houses along the Promenade did a good job, as far as conservationists are concerned, in containing the seasonal pilgrimage to the sea. Populations in such towns expanded hugely during the season. Nowadays, the preference is for self-catering holidays and consequently the demand for camping, caravan or holiday chalet-type developments has increased substantially. Everyone wants to be as near the sea as possible and the outskirts of Weymouth, towards Osmington, show the result. Very large caravan parks and a holiday camp are prominent features of the landscape. The openness of the undulating downland makes these sort of features very difficult to screen effectively.

Between Kimmeridge and Lulworth Cove stretch the army gunnery ranges. They occupy some 11 kilometres (seven miles) of outstanding coastal landscape. The army's presence in the area was greatly extended during the emergency of the last war. A wide variety of weapons are used and the proximity of the large naval port at Portland allows combined services operations. The village settlement at Tyneham was cleared and its shell-shattered ruins are still visible. Over recent years, there has been a gradual

Army gunners made short shrift of the farmsteads of Tyneham. The area is closed to the public for most of the year

Above: Where the prairies meet the sea – the Norman Chapel on St Aldhelm's Head surrounded by a sea of wheat, stark contrast to the richness of wild flora

Below: Looking west from St Aldhelm's Head towards Kimmeridge – geological diversity contributes to outstanding scenery and great wildlife interest

improvement in access arrangements for the public, most importantly to allow the use of the coast path during weekends over most of the year and during the holiday weeks of the school year. Some credit is claimed by supporters of the army usage that restricted access and prohibition of certain farming activities have ensured the survival of some endangered plant species. On the other hand, archaeologists are very concerned about the extent of damage 70-ton tanks and 155-mm high-explosive shells can do to the great number of antiquities within the ranges.

At Kimmeridge is found what has until recently been a strange sight in the British countryside, the 'nodding donkey' oil pump. Kimmeridge clay has yielded a combustible oil for many years and cliffs in the area have burst into spontaneous fire and smouldered for long periods. Oil extracted from the shales was also used for early street lighting in Paris, of all places. Today, the oil exploration is penetrating far deeper strata. British Petroleum recently published plans for fifty on-shore drilling sites and it seems very likely that commercially useful reserves of oil will be tapped in this area on-shore, and possibly from oil rigs stationed off-shore.

The Heritage Coast concept has achieved a number of things so far. First, it has supplemented the concerns of the National Trust and focused popular concern on the general problem of preserving our coastal heritage.

Secondly, the introduction of long-distance paths along the coast, which now stretch from Studland virtually around the south-west peninsula to the Bristol Channel, have greatly improved access and provided a waymarked route along which many thousands of people can wander at their will.

The noticeboards which are found along the path explain the importance of features which have contributed to making the area a Heritage Coast. It seems doubtful that access for the public over the army ranges at Lulworth could have been achieved quite as soon if there had been no organisation to help plan and advise on the establishment of such arrangements. Access, however, is limited and this points to one very fundamental weakness in the whole Heritage Coast programme; it is designed to co-ordinate essentially voluntary co-operation by the important interested parties in the area. The coastline is, as already stated, apart from the National Trust lands, largely in the hands of long-established family estates. Their protective stewardship of the area together with their ownership of most access roads to the coast has been in no small part responsible for maintaining the undeveloped appearance of much of the landscape.

Although likely to continue, their protection is by no means a statutory one and pressures on estates for commercial development are ever present in today's economic climate.

The constraints of planning laws as exercised by the local authority can be seen as some safeguard but these laws have the weakness of the 1947 Act

A 'nodding donkey' pumps oil out of the Kimmeridge Shales. Today the Dorset Coast is poised for much greater oil exploration

generally, in that they exclude agriculture and forestry – and thus a potential threat exists to distinctive indigenous flora and fauna and to a characteristic landscape.

Conservation bodies are many and fragmented. They attempt to exercise some influence but woefully lack resources and manpower. Some are financed through the local authority with Countryside Commission money – the Heritage Coast wardens, for example. Their task is to manage on the ground competing interests and ensure a harmonious accommodation of all pursuits.

In conclusion, it is difficult not to recall the policy statement of the National Trust – that only ownership by the Trust could ensure inalienable protection for the coastal heritage. It is worth speculating how effectively the *ad hoc* arrangements of the Heritage Coast concept, however laudable in principle, would stand up to concerted efforts to develop part of this unique coastline.

This fierce-looking denizen of the deep – a long-spined sea scorpion – is common in Dorset's marine nature reserve at Kimmeridge

The traditional seaside town. The Promenade hotels and guest houses have increasingly lost out to self-catering caravanners and campers. Weymouth, Dorset

The fossil forest at Lulworth – one of the many spectacular geological gems of this Heritage coastline

But a concern for the unsurpassed qualities of the east Dorset coast should not blind us to the fact that there are still other areas of our coastline that must not be neglected or abandoned to the developer. For example, across from Studland and beyond Bournemouth are the soft brown sandy cliffs that run from Christchurch harbour to Hurst Castle opposite the Needles of the Isle of Wight. Although much of the cliff top has been built upon, considerable open space remains, whilst the beaches below are almost wholly available for recreation. Such areas, in very close proximity to large population centres, offer considerable opportunities for the creation of better visitor facilities, so taking the pressure off those wilder parts of the coast we would wish to protect particularly against such incursions.

Perhaps there remains a need for a total policy framework for our coastline which recognises it as a special, unique resource calling for a coherent and co-ordinated approach which embraces all the demands made upon it.

Chapter 8
The Last Ditch

WATER, to man, is a hostile environment. Although essential to any productive life, it has traditionally caused devastation and tragedy on a scale probably greater than any other natural element. Controlled and channelled it has given societies enormous benefits and centuries of technology have been applied to effect this control. In this, as in other spheres of man's endeavour, the twentieth century has seen the greatest increase in man's potential.

To many species of flora and fauna, however, the unrestricted interplay of water, land and air provide a diversity of habitats which they are uniquely equipped to survive in.

There is, therefore, an inherent conflict between man's continued preoccupation with making his environment safe and productive and the very survival of plant and dependent animal species in habitats congenial to them.

The 'wetlands' of Britain historically have provided one of the most critical points of contact between man and his environment. Until relatively recent times greater areas were prone to water domination, either through dramatic sea incursions, periodic riverine flooding or chronically bad drainage. However, the natural 'wetlands' of Britain have shrunk steadily for centuries, until today mere vestiges remain of what was once a common habitat for plants and dependent creatures. More accurately, there was not a uniform habitat but a whole diversity of ecological conditions where the presence of water, permanently or sporadically, saline or fresh, was critical in determining the vegetation.

The habitats range from conventional bodies of freshwater lakes and rivers, through a whole succession of water meadows, fens, bogs, grazing marshes, to salt-water marshes, mud flats, estuaries and areas along low-lying shorelines.

Historically they proved among the most inaccessible and agriculturally unproductive areas for man. They were mysterious areas, often accompanied by dangers real or imaginary, and if the marshes of Cambridgeshire provided refuge for Hereward the Wake, they continued for centuries after to provide sanctuary to an enormous variety of plant and wildlife species.

The expansion and development of agricultural land is almost synonymous with that of drainage. Early farmers cultivated the thin sandy and chalky soils of England before tackling the heavier clays and progressively

The East Coast storm surge of 1953 – Canadian airmen help Norfolk farmers repair the breached embankments along the River Waveney. This disaster had far-reaching effects on the marshland countryside

draining the fens and marshes. Where technology could master the task of pumping away the water and so lowering the water table, the resultant land was often extremely fertile and by definition flat – offering no natural obstacles to extensive, highly-mechanised farming. The landscape of much of Lincolnshire and Cambridgeshire is testament to this, where the only barriers are the drainage ditches and dykes themselves.

Such are the rewards, agriculturally, that often elaborate and highly-expensive drainage schemes can be undertaken. These developments are often encouraged and supported by schemes to improve river drainage and flood-prevention schemes. The latter often have access to considerable public funds and, as we shall see in Halvergate Marshes of Norfolk, public funds can lead to considerable private profit.

The much-publicised devastation of the 1953 east coast floods seems to have had a cathartic effect on public opinion in Britain. As a direct result, enormous public works of flood prevention have been undertaken. The increasing embankment of river channels and the prevention of the natural run-off of water over river washlands has culminated with the need to protect areas like central London with the gigantic Thames Barrage.

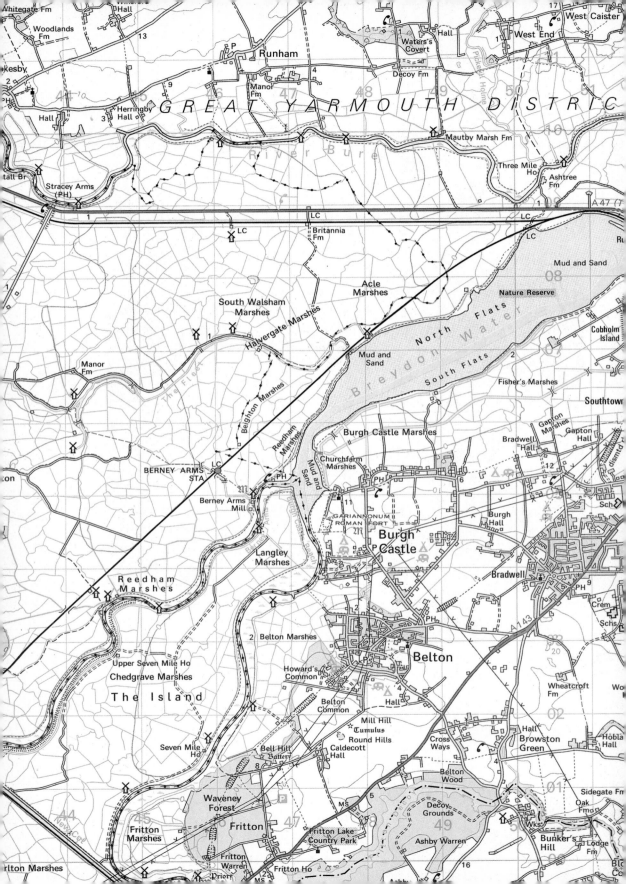

Reedmarsh and windpumps. A unique, subtle and vulnerable landscape. Part of our countryside heritage which should not be allowed to disappear

Map 7 *Norfolk Broadland*

The mosaic of dykes between the raised levels of the Broadland rivers converge at their outlet to the sea at Yarmouth. The landscape is dotted with the remains of windpumps which traditionally drained the marshes. The rivers are tidal and the Yare still provides a navigation twenty miles inland to Norwich.

Like the farmers who live on the slopes of Mount Vesuvius and Etna, people have always calculated a risk in gaining their livelihood against possible natural catastrophe. In the case of wetlands, in England, that occasional risk of flooding with its attendant but temporary dangers to life and property has been reduced by enormous public expenditure. In human terms alone, the cost benefits are doubtful; in terms of the destruction of considerable areas of distinctive habitat, the loss is incalculable.

It may be argued that man's survival in all manner of difficult environments has been at the cost of subjugating and destroying nature. Indeed, the Darwinian theory of evolution may now make progress as a process of man's determination of what habitats survive. In the area of Norfolk's Broadland, we can see these forces at work today.

The irony of the Norfolk Broads is that they are man-made – a direct result of the flooding of medieval peat workings. The paradox is that while the 'natural' wetlands of Britain were drained, ploughed and sown, some compensation occurred as a result of the abandonment of mineral workings, and other industrial engineering enterprises. As Bryn Green has written:

> Industry has been responsible for creating most of the open waters in Lowland Britain – Britain's canal network contributed over 4800 kilometres [about 3000 miles] of waterway with some 100 reservoirs to feed them. These reservoirs alone occupy nearly 2000 hectares [4942 acres] – reservoirs for water supply, hydroelectric schemes and other water consumptive industrial needs have added further to the total.[27]

Green estimates there are 'at least 750 water bodies over two hectares [around five acres] in size as a result of sand and gravel extraction alone'. On a more prosaic scale, he further states that historically

> . . . village and farm ponds of which there was once at least one in every field in some parts of the country, were dug or dammed to water stock, or to mine calcareous strata as marl for liming the fields. Fish or stew ponds provided an important source of protein, mill ponds and hammer ponds drove machinery, and moats and lakes defended or beautified large homes and estates. *ibid*

It has been contended that there is a case for *preserving* certain distinctive landscapes against *any* development whatsoever. The rationale for this rests on certain fundamental assumptions, not least that there are unique habitats for flora and fauna which once lost are lost forever. The loss of the habitats will lead to the extinction of certain plants and animal species, the consequences of which cannot be foreseen and should not be allowed. These habitats are increasingly threatened by activities such as farming which if 'totally environmentally costed' are marginally unnecessary.

Of the Broadland region E. A. Ellis wrote:

The vegetation of this area today comprises a magnificent series of aquatic and fen communities, fuller and richer than that surviving in any other part of Britain. The waters hold species of charophytes and the Stagshorn weed (*Naias Marina*) unknown elsewhere in these islands. The Broads are the chief remaining home of plants like the Water Soldier and Cowbane, and nowhere else are there such massive ranks of the tall Marsh Sowthistle along miles of riverside. The Fen Orchid and Round Leaved Wintergreen linger in the mossy fens and the Great Spearwort raises its yellow heads between the reeds. Plants of ancient lineage in these eastern valleys hold their places in the everchanging pattern of swamp and carr. In the humid shelter of tall marsh vegetation, countless little fungi thrive almost as in a tropical jungle, attacking plants alive and dead and parasiting millions of insects and spiders . . . The waters, because of their varying salinity, support a remarkable range of planktonic animals, including many curiously specialised crustaceans, and freshwater polyzoa flourish greatly. The more calcareous regions are very rich in molluscs and the riversides yield an interesting series of brackish-water species along their lower regions. The insects include the British Swallowtail butterfly, surviving in abundance nowhere else, and two dragonflies which are restricted to this region. The beds of reeds, sedge and rush are haunts of many rare and local moths especially the Wainscots, and as recently as 1961, a new British Footman (*Pelosia obtusa*) was found near one of the Broads. Whereas most of the ancient fenland of Cambridgeshire, Huntingdonshire and Lincolnshire has been drained out of existence, almost all its specialised insects and other invertebrates, as well as its plants are represented in the broadland region.[28]

Ellis's description conjures up a picture of a primeval 'soup' habitat and was based largely on the position in Broadland in the late 1950s. Much has since been lost. The sixties saw an unprecedented increase in holiday traffic, particularly in the large motor cruisers which poured untreated sewage and other effluents into the water of the Broads and rivers. Water quality and quantity are the most critical elements in the entire ecosystem and both were to suffer.

Controls were eventually put on the discharge coming from boats on the Broads but much damage due to eutrophication or an increase of nitrates and other elements had been done. In addition, the full trauma of the 1953 floods was still working its way through in the form of increased drainage schemes, river embankment and the lowering of water tables. Hectares of land which had been subject to the rhythmical wash of rejuvenating flood water were

The Swallowtail butterfly, a species unique to Broadland marshes. Only constant habitat management ensures its food supply and its survival

Richer aquatic plantlife than in any other area of Britain: a healthy dyke in Norfolk's Broadland. Drainage improvements desiccate these habitats
Right: Human competition for the waterways. Horning Ferry, Norfolk

The rapid increase in holiday traffic, especially large motor cruisers, in the sixties posed an ever-greater threat to the ecology of the Broads and rivers

now piped, pumped and their pastures 'improved', or even worse, from the naturalist viewpoint, given over to cereal cultivation.

The Halvergate Marshes of Norfolk provide a classic case of how profound countryside change can be effected. Its grazing marshes are the most extensive still left in Britain. They are the matrix into which even more specialised habitats of reed swamp and fen are set.

Charged with its statutory obligation to render safe the land from flooding and improve its natural drainage, the Internal Drainage Boards have instituted many schemes. The windpumps, the dominant picturesque features of the landscape, had long been defunct; their function of pumping water up from the marshes into the embanked rivers had been superseded first by steam, then by oil and later by electrically-driven machinery whose operation was not dependent on the caprice of East Anglian winds and therefore was continuous and remorseless in its operation when water levels required it.

Later generations of water pump, notably based on the Archimedean screw principle, had phenomenal capacity. Nowadays an innocuous building at Stokesby houses the outlet end of such a twin-screw device. It can pump eighty tons of water a minute into the higher levels of the River Bure and its effects are felt on the drainage of land 32 kilometres (20 miles) distant.

Such technology allowed for the first time the reality of not only maintaining the water level to prevent flooding, but of effectively lowering it.

As a result, many plant and animal communities were left high and dry and their extinction over vast areas was now inevitable. The position was further compounded by the associated effect of metalled all-weather roads the Internal Drainage Boards had built over the marshes to facilitate the construction and maintenance of their new pumping stations. These allowed the local farmers to get the new mechanical monsters of the agricultural industry onto the newly-drained land. Cereal cultivation with the active encouragement of government and EEC subsidies was an added incentive to the increase in profitability of the erstwhile grazing marshes.

Farmers are also paid subsidies for any drainage improvement schemes they undertake; the law at the moment allows payment retrospectively for the work being done. Schemes do not need the formal approval of the Ministry of Agriculture before being undertaken, and payment is guaranteed.

The economics of the agricultural change in the Halvergate Marshes has been calculated by one conservation organisation, Friends of the Earth, who are implacably opposed to their conversion to arable. They estimate that with all the subsidies available for drainage and land improvement, together with funds channelled through the Internal Drainage Boards for flood protection, there is a potential investment of £800 of public money per hectare (£324 per acre). They further estimate that once converted, the land will yield £100 per hectare (£40 per acre) per year more under cereals than as grazing marsh and that some farmers have more than 800 hectares (2000 acres) which could be converted.

Friends of the Earth also claim that the Internal Drainage Boards are like private clubs, most of the members being large farmers, solicitors, land agents or others who have a vested interest in land values.

The Wildlife and Countryside Act 1981 in fact allows for intervention by bodies like the Nature Conservancy Council who will pay farmers *not* to improve their land in order to attempt the preservation of important endangered habitats. The problem here is one of timing, as intervention is often too late, though the funds available for purchasing the respite on an annual basis are pitifully small. Only a microscopic part of the areas considered under thread could be safeguarded in this way. If the position remains unchanged, it seems that very little can actually save the destruction of a unique wetland ecosystem.

On small isolated reserves, the Nature Conservancy Council, together with the Norfolk County Naturalist Trust and with the co-operation of the local

Overleaf: Glimpses of the past way of life can still be seen on nature reserves today. Management by the Nature Conservancy Council attempts to reproduce the old Broadland habitats. Ranworth, Norfolk

landowners, have set about preserving vestiges of the old Fenland habitats. Paradoxically, as a result of the general lowering of water tables, and the drastically deteriorated water quality, these reserves are only possible with the active management of the area. Water is often pumped in and dammed to maintain a high water level.

In such a reserve at Woodbastwick, noticeboard displays illustrate how nature itself would have, through various stages in ecological succession, transformed open water into a series of vegetations, culminating after many years in oak forest. That this did not happen over large areas of English Fenland was due, of course, to man's interference and to the previously traditional economy these areas supported.

The photographs of J. Payne Jennings, P. H. Emerson and George Christopher Davies splendidly evoke the past landscape of Broadland which was the ultimate expression of the interplay of man's endeavours with the distinctive flora and fauna of these areas.[29]

As we have seen in other landscapes, once the economic base of the countryside changes, the landscape will alter irrevocably unless a managed intervention is undertaken. In the case of Britain's wetlands, the loss in both wildlife and landscape terms would be very great indeed.

Reed harvesting – part of the traditional livelihood of the marshlands. The care of reed beds was an important element in preserving the wildlife and landscape

Above: 'Cattle at Noontide on the Bure' by J. Payne Jennings. *Below*: 'Gathering Water Lilies' by P. H. Emerson. Two pictures by the famous nineteenth-century photographers which splendidly evoke the charm of the traditional Broadland landscape. Here Man and Nature worked in harmony

The situation in Halvergate and Broadland in general is so critical that the Countryside Commission wishes to see a much more powerful body set up to plan the future for the region. The present Broads Authority lacks the statutory powers to intervene in land management, navigation, water quality and conservation, although it has tried strenuously to persuade the organisations who currently hold these powers to exercise them in order to conserve the landscape and amenity.

A windpump, once common over much of England's fens and marshes. In Broadland they still contribute to a distinctive landscape
Right: The brooding landscape of Breydon Water, Norfolk

Wildfowling: the popularity of this sport with local landowners helps maintain the wetlands from other developments

Some have argued for a Broadland National Park but the type of legislation under consideration by Norfolk and Suffolk County Councils would stop short of such a designation. It remains to be seen whether these moves can be realised in time. So far Broadland has lost one-fifth of its grazing marsh. The area constitutes nearly a quarter of this type of habitat in the country and its significance is greater than that, for nowhere else apart from Halvergate do we see such a unique landscape in a large contiguous block.

There are, however, some signs that this irreplaceable part of our landscape heritage may be preserved. Recently, and for the first time ever, the Department of the Environment has indicated it will take planning powers to preserve areas of marshland in the Halvergate from conversion to arable farming. This somewhat belated show of concern is one hopeful sign although it is being looked at warily by conservation groups. It may be only a flash in the pan or a token intervention. Most concerned parties now urgently want to see a much stronger body constituted as a successor to the Broads Authority.

There are other wetland vestiges in Britain where concern has led to controversy and where similar powers of conservation may be needed. The Somerset Levels are fine grazing marshes under constant threat of improvement. Other vestiges are found in the Ainsdale Marshes of Lancashire and in what is left of the old Yorkshire *ings*, a feature which is incorporated in place names like Pickering in the North Riding.

The main problem in all such areas is the survival of a landscape which was the expression of a past economy maintained by rural practices long since gone. This is not a problem unique to Britain. Over much of Europe we see a continual struggle for survival of 'traditional' landscapes which are being overwhelmed by modern commercial needs. In France with a similar population to our own, but a countryside nearly three times as big, there is also concern to protect not only the habitat of flora and fauna, but in some selected areas the entire human rural economy and lifestyle that contributed to the distinctive landscape, or 'pays' as the French call it.

It is to this consideration we turn next.

Chapter 9
Parc De Paysan

THE journey in mid-June from Béziers or Montpellier in France along the N9 and across the narrow lowland plain of the Mediterranean northwards to Millau, on the southern edge of the Parc National des Cévennes, is not scenically a striking experience, except perhaps in the latter stages. For much of the way, the slow upward climb is barely perceptible and one is impressed more by the characteristic vegetation of olive trees and vines, the wayside stalls selling cherries and early peaches and the heat of the morning sun. Beyond Millau and heading on first north and then east along the 58 kilometres (36 miles) to Florac in the heart of the national park, one is not only now aware of the sharpness of the air, for the road lies at over 366 metres (1200 feet) above sea-level, but the rapid plunge into a vast chasm whose walls rise on either side a further 487 metres (1600 feet) above the River Tarn, casting deep shadows into the gorge.

The river, now a pale reflection of its former self, once cut deep down into the horizontally bedded Jurassic limestone in the aftermath of the last great glaciation some 10,000 years ago, to create one of the most spectacular scenic attractions in Europe. It is a Grand Canyon on a smaller and more intimate scale, rather than anything that resembles Cheddar Gorge in Somerset, although geologically it has more to do with the latter than with the former. Larger settlements deep at the foot of the gorge are few, but occasionally small villages cling to the steep valley sides. Wherever the slope and aspect allow, mixed stands of trees – oak, chestnut and pine – are in evidence, and here and there from these areas of forest dozens of small terraces have been cut. Some are still used to grow vines or vegetables, some show recent signs of having been cut for hay, but most are overgrown and abandoned to the profusion of wild flowers that are so strikingly in evidence at this time of year both in the gorge and on the plateau-like top of the limestone massif of the Causse Méjean on either side. Everywhere, but especially on the high causse, the variety of the flora is quite overwhelming even though the enormous swathes of yellow-flowered broom dominate the scene.

But limestone is not the only bedrock from which the whole area has been carved. If one climbs from the foot of the valley up the D63 road from Florac which rapidly ascends the eastern escarpment of the limestone to the edge of

Left: Settlements growing out of the limestone walls of the Gorge du Tarn

the plateau, it is possible to see from such a vantage point the other formations of which the region consists.

Immediately to the north-east, one is aware of the very highest point in the area, that of Mont Lozère. This is a windswept granite upland, over 1800 metres (6000 feet) at its highest and with its broad, smoothly rounded shoulders broken only by the occasional outcropping tor. Its lack of trees and its acid-loving plantlife together with its terrain are reminiscent of Dartmoor. Below the cold, bleak moorlands at heights less than 1400 metres (4500 feet) the slopes of the land are covered with pines, spruce and fir, eventually giving way to mixed stands of conifers, oak, beech and sweet chestnut. Lower still, at around 450 metres (1500 feet) and less, lie steeply-wooded valleys in which deciduous trees predominate.

Above: Mont Lozère landscape. Its granite tor features are similar to those on the windswept face of Dartmoor
Left: Terraces from countless past cultivations etched into the arid limestone. Clearly in the past the peasant population was much greater in this region

Above: Under the escarpment of the Causse Méjean, the Château in Florac, now
headquarters of the Parc National des Cévennes authorities
Right: Old terraces amidst the chestnut forest of the Gardon Valleys

The softer countryside of the Gardon Valleys – a hidden, secret landscape

Surrounding such massive granite upwellings as the Lozère are great haloes of metamorphic rock. Perhaps the most striking of these areas lie to the east and south of Florac and they are known as the Gardon Valleys. A greater contrast with the upland granites could hardly be imagined, for here the schists of the bedrock have weathered into a series of valleys. The 'feel' of this area with its heavily-wooded slopes on which the chestnut and mulberry predominate, its terraced smallholdings, its tiny hamlets and small isolated farmsteads, each as if it were part of an intimate jigsaw, is one of warmth and friendliness. It radiates a kindly atmosphere not at all in evidence on the Lozère or on the windswept rocky plateau of the high causse. Indeed the profusion of terraced vines even suggests a softer climate redolent of the Mediterranean that lies to the immediate south of this upland region.

Delightful as such a visit can be in a month when a countryside already notable for its variety and beauty is enhanced by a display of wild flowers that can scarcely be matched elsewhere in western Europe, what is its real relevance in a book about the countryside of England and Wales?

The answer lies simply in the fact that many of the previous chapters have emphasised the need to manage and conserve the rural environment, particularly in those areas where the landscape is of rare or unique quality. How this has been done and in whose interests are not matters fixed for all time. These must remain open to debate and could eventually lead in new policy directions. Indeed, the debate on the British uplands initiated by the

Countryside Commission in 1983 bears witness to this. It is, therefore, relevant to look at how other nations approach these questions and this is why we turn in this chapter to our nearest neighbour, France, to look at one of their national parks, that of the Cévennes.

Of the five such designated areas in France, it is particularly appropriate that we should consider this upland region. This is because it demonstrates a sequence of events all too familiar to us from the chapters on Snowdonia and the Lake District where the economics of the 1970s and 1980s have overtaken farm systems designed to cope with the late nineteenth-century conditions. Here, as in those upland areas of Wales and England, small family farms, usually dependent on stock-rearing in a comparatively harsh environment and often well away from the large population centres, find that the prices they receive for what they manage to produce have been outstripped by rising costs and the vagaries of the market, notwithstanding EEC and state support policies. The younger members of the family often cannot be supported by the farm and have to seek work elsewhere; indeed, even the farmer himself may look to supplement his income if he is not to be faced with declining living standards and the ultimate indignity of being forced to abandon his way of life. In situations such as this, the landscape must suffer and what was the outcome of years of sound farming practice is quickly lost in a welter of overgrown pastures, derelict farm buildings and dilapidated stone walls. As

Above: Open to the elements, a farmstead in an abandoned village of the Cévennes
Overleaf: Meadows of wild narcissi. June in the pastures of Mont Lozère

the farmers move out, the fabric of the community at large deteriorates since services such as public transport, local schools and shops can no longer be supported. Some might argue in favour of such change since it increases the extent of what is truly wild, or conversely maintain that one socio-economic way of life should, if it is no longer appropriate, be succeeded by another, such as forestry, which will offer a reasonable return on investment. But this is not the policy pursued in such areas of France as the Parc National des Cévennes.

Here, as in other French national parks, the maintenance of a population of sufficient size to support the traditional landscape is central to its philosophy. This is so even if in the heart of the park (an area of 89,000 hectares or nearly 220,000 acres) the population of some 2000 has fallen in twenty years to around 500, mainly living and working on about 120 farms. For each of the three zones we have identified within the park, this policy is articulated in different ways. However, nowhere is the temptation to introduce new forms of economic activity acceded to. For example, although the Lozère area might lend itself to commercial forestry which would require an increase in the stands of conifers almost certainly planted in 'serried ranks', the policy has been to discourage and in some areas forbid such practices. Clear felling is not allowed and even mechanisation of the maintenance and extraction of the mixed timber stands that currently exist is not permitted. All timber is

A 'Berger' or shepherd of the Haute Causse leads his flock. Sheepmeat from such flocks faces strong competition from farmers in Britain

felled and removed by traditional methods using horses, in spite of its inefficiency and expense. Natural tree regeneration is encouraged with some supplementary replanting. Whatever economic opportunities have been foregone here (and it should be added that non-plantation timber of this kind fetches a premium on the market), the object of the national park is to manage the area in perpetuity as a semi-natural mixed broad-leaved/coniferous forest, a situation which strongly contrasts with that of our own national parks.

In the Lozère area, conditions for agriculture are at their most difficult as a result of climate and terrain. Farms are very small, with livestock holdings specialising in cattle for meat and milk production, and sheep entirely bred for meat. Although there is the normal EEC support system for such farms, the park authority offers a great deal of additional assistance to improve the farmers' lot. Holdings have been purchased in order to redistribute land in units of greater viability, whilst others have been bought and then leased out again to farmers at a rent which reflects the desire of the authority to ensure the maintenance of landscape standards and regional wildlife. For example, the need to maintain the buttresses of the terraced areas, as well as stone walls and the traditional irrigation channels which are such a special characteristic of pasture land in the Lozère, is very much reflected in the lower rents demanded of tenants and the availability of grants to cover these activities for

Farmer and grandson: few expect the peasant way of life can continue without massive government assistance

owner-occupiers. In England and Wales, only the management of the National Trust on equivalent tenant holdings, such as that of John Allen in the Hartsop Valley, seems in any way to parallel such an approach. The differences between the efforts of a private trust in a national park operating in a piecemeal fashion compared with those of a state-backed park authority must be at once apparent and hardly need underlining.

The problems of agriculture on the Causse Méjean and its relationship to the landscape are of a somewhat different order. Indeed the very success of sheep farming as a result of the increase in the amount of lamb consumed in France and the buoyant demand for Roquefort cheese made from sheep's milk which now fetches a premium price, has led to the over-grazing of the sward on the comparatively thin soils of this limestone plateau. In an area so heavily dependent on agriculture, the park authority views with anxiety the possibility of the fragile boom coming to a sudden end (perhaps through the import of cheaper UK lamb) and the fact that there is still some evidence of continuing rural depopulation. Should sheep farming decline, these uplands would undoubtedly revert to scrub and thorn; failing that, the pressure to pursue commercial forestry might become overwhelming. Thus in an effort to maintain the present situation, the park authority with the government have supported the construction of new in-wintering buildings, a very

Above: Maturing Roquefort cheese, made from the milk of ewes from the limestone plateaux of this part of France
Left: Depopulation of the countryside. The village of L'Hôpital, once a community of 200, today has only a few seasonal visitors

necessary adjunct to an effective sheep-farming system in a harsh winter climate. These are made from local materials and are positioned with due respect to the local landscape.

If the contrast between the high causse and the Gardon Valleys could not be more marked physically, they also differ greatly in terms of their economic bases. The terrain and the climate of the latter favoured the development of a once complex economy. This was founded on sweet chestnuts which provided a staple food for humans and their farmstock (sheep, goats, pigs and a few cows) and some income from their sale. This was supplemented in the nineteenth century by the development of silk production as a cottage industry based on the planting of mulberry trees. This activity died in the twentieth century along with the importance of the sweet chestnut. In its wake it left an economy based only on goat and sheep rearing. This in turn set in motion a process of depopulation which continued until the 1970s. Then with the establishment of the national park, the link between landscape and the local economy was at last recognised.

The reaction of the park authority was to encourage only the kind of hill-top forestry that would complement the landscape and for those farmers who remained to build up their stock numbers to a more viable level. At the same time grant aid was offered to those who wished to construct winter quarters for their stock. It also encouraged part-time forestry work for these farmers, but most useful of all has been the financial support for the conversion of unwanted cottages and barns into holiday homes or 'gîtes'. Whilst maintaining traditional external appearances these offer the holidaymaker the highest standards of accommodation. Thus the average farmer in the area might now find his income made up in almost equal parts from money brought in by the letting of his gîtes (handled by a central agency), his work in the forest and the income from his stock. Although such a system cannot be expected to support an extended family – and sons and daughters leave for the cities – the outward drift has been stemmed. Today, when a holding of the kind discussed becomes available, there are always newcomers anxious to take over. There does indeed now seem to be evidence to support the national park's contention that the policies will ensure 'the schist dweller will live and die in the shade of the chestnut tree'.

But just as the support given to the retention of an older economic order and way of life differs so markedly from any existing philosophy in the national parks of England and Wales, so do other aspects of the organisation of national parks here and in France. These are most obvious in the structure of a two-tier organisation which identifies an inner or central zone for a park (in the case of the Cévennes, 89,000 hectares or 220,000 acres) and a peripheral zone around this (128,000 hectares or 316,000 acres). There is often little to choose between the two in terms of the beauty of the landscape;

the criterion for the split is population density. Thus, in the Cévennes, the central zone contains no more than twenty-five families and has the least disturbed landscape. No new construction is permitted within it unless required for agricultural purposes. Even the renovation of existing buildings requires special permission. Access by car is strictly regulated, camping prohibited, whilst there is complete protection for all flora and fauna. Only minor modifications to forest management plans are allowed.

The peripheral zone, containing around 61,000 people as opposed to the 528 in the central zone, acts as a buffer and contains a number of small-scale industries as well as agriculture and the services required by the tourist. The contrast here with the situation in England and Wales is at once apparent; national parks were chosen primarily for their overall landscape qualities and happen to include quite substantial settlements, as well as other activities such as quarrying, military training, water collection, power generation and forestry. Indeed, in the period since their designation, many such activities have been allowed to expand considerably and it has been thought quite appropriate to add to some parks nuclear power stations, potash mines and radar early warning systems. In spite of the absence of any such activities in France, the concept of its two-tier national park is, however, not without its advocates in Britain. In fact, it was proposed in 1979 by the Countryside Review Committee (a group made up entirely from civil servants with a departmental concern for rural matters), but it has so far not found official favour as we stated in Chapter 2.

In addition to a whole range of bye-laws and regulations which have the authority of the French parliament and which have been designed to protect landscape, wildlife and the economy of national parks, perhaps the most significant contrast with the British situation is to be found in the budget and staff provisions. Even allowing for the fact that the Parc National des Cévennes has a total area well over forty per cent greater than the Lake District, our largest park, in terms of comparative finance it is very considerably better off than its British counterparts. Its most recent annual grant was well in excess of one million francs, *for the development of policy objectives alone*. The officers of the park, headed by a director, number about sixty and include thirty managerial, administrative and technical employees and thirty field staff, including inspectors, regional heads and wardens. In addition the park supports a comprehensive programme of research which is in the hands of groups of professional foresters, biologists, zoologists, geographers and architects. And as if this were not enough, an advisory committee of seventy nominated members from the three departments in which the national park lies promote 'the development of the park aided by state-based inter-ministerial finance'. We need but compare this with the resources available to the Lake District National Park Authority where it shares the £6.8 million *in total* which not only finances all *ten* national parks, but is also used to provide support for the thirty-three Areas of Outstanding Natural Beauty (AONBs), as well as long-distance footpaths, country parks, the Heritage Coasts, etc.

In terms of staffing, the Lake District Park Authority has, at comparable levels with the Cévennes authority, less than two-thirds of its numbers and though its 'advisory committee' performs a somewhat different range of functions, it is only half the size of its French counterpart. Moreover, the Lake District Park Authority supports no equivalent programme of research into matters related to its ecology.

It is then hardly surprising that much of the excellent literature about the Parc National des Cévennes, available from its head office in Florac, exudes self-confidence. The park authority clearly believes it is winning the battle to preserve the right balance between fauna, flora, man's cultural heritage and the economic prosperity of the region, and it is instructive that it concludes that visitors are only its secondary concern, since the well-being of the permanent inhabitants takes first priority. Any conversation with a local park official puts the 'strengthening of the inhabitants' simple joy of living here

Reared in captivity, Griffin Vultures, once native to the Cévennes, have now been successfully re-established in the Parc

and working here' by 'encouraging the villages to recover a spirit of communal life' top of any list of priorities. It is up to the visitor who comes to enjoy the park also to understand the way of life. Clearly the park authorities believe that the concept of *genre de vie* is alive and well, at least in the Cévennes. Whilst a cautious view should be taken of the longer-term success of such ideas, since they depend on the maintenance of a viable level of population in the park – and after all, abandoned farmsteads are much in evidence in the Cévennes – the existence of these policies in this French context must lead us to ask whether similar approaches would be of value in our own National Parks. If so, would the resources available here be remotely adequate in such changed policy circumstances?

Whatever your response, and it is easy to be cynical, it is only too evident that the original concept of the national park in Britain as suggested by John Dower in 1944 has been far from realised. Additionally, the powers that national park authorities in Britain have are largely in the form of the preparation of a general structure plan and the exercise of development controls, either of which may be overriden by the Secretary of State for the Environment. His insistence that the A66 road improvement scheme go ahead inside the Lake District National Park, in spite of the opposition of its planning board, is but one example of such a situation. More important still is the fact that unlike the French national parks, where finance is available to support traditional farming systems, our national parks have little control over an agriculture support system which is applied across the board. Hence the damage to Exmoor through the availability of grants for ploughing it up, to its immense ecological detriment and without any reference to these moorlands' special status of being within a national park. And, then again, in terms of the protection of flora and fauna in Britain, powers are not vested with the park authorities as in France, but such as they are, with the Nature Conservancy Council through the auspices of the Wildlife and Countryside Act of 1981. Where the British park authorities are concerned, perhaps it is not unfair to postulate that their only significant claim to total effectiveness is in the provision of a warden service and general information to assist visitors and diminish the possibility of conflict between them and other interests within the park. But compared with the national park authorities in France, one is certainly left to doubt whether their English and Welsh counterparts can make a significant contribution over matters of real and fundamental importance. Even the simplest of attempts to marry upland farming with good conservation practice has seen the two elements not *intrinsically related* as the French do. Rather it has been left to the Countryside Commission to do what it can by way of advice through its Upland Management Scheme against a tide of factors pushing farmers in quite another direction.

Chapter 10
Views of a Valley

THE dominant first impression one forms of the Stonor or Hambleden valleys is how remarkably well-wooded they are. This impression, moreover, is a true one. Unlike some of the English southern shires where healthy hedgerows still beguile the eye and leave you thinking you are on the edge of a great wood, here, on the Chilterns, there actually are woods and big ones.

The map shows the extent of the woodland in this part of Oxfordshire and Buckinghamshire; it occupies perhaps over a third of the land area and the skilful rambler can walk many miles under the cover of trees.

Woods have an emotional appeal to many people. In some they evoke fear, in others a welcome feeling of seclusion and mystery. It is hard to walk deep into these woods without triggering memories of long-forgotten childhood tales like The Dark Wood of *Wind in the Willows*, and indeed Kenneth Grahame did live in Pangbourne, situated on the Thames-side edge of the Chilterns.

Historic legends often feature great forests – most notably Robin Hood – but many fugitives have found sanctuary in the English woods and even today occasional stories emerge of individuals who hide away from modern society to enjoy a spartan life in a makeshift forest shelter. For those who have not lost the art, survival in a deciduous woodland can be a sustainable challenge.

That the imagination can race on in such fashion in a tract of country barely 56 kilometres (35 miles) from London seems a curious anomaly – how have the Chilterns remained such a relatively isolated area when counties far further afield have been systematically developed?

The isolation of this area has always been a feature of its history.

There are archaeological remains of Roman villas at Bix and at several places along the Thames near Hambleden and Mill End. The river was the favoured means of communication through the area, thereby avoiding the traditionally hazardous route over the Chilterns towards Oxford. The original forest is described as an inhospitable thicket of thorn, yew and juniper. The departure of the Romans left the Chilterns a bastion of the British; even the Saxons left large areas of the Chilterns alone, preferring to bypass the thin chalky hills with their flint outcrops, to develop the more amenable farmlands of the Midlands. The Saxons took over Dorchester as their main crossing of the Thames upstream from Reading whilst the British

Hidden within the hedgerows are the old pathways, used for generations until the motor roads produced a new network in the countryside

made use of Wallingford – its name being a derivative of ford of the 'wealhs' (or British).

There is some evidence that so isolated was the area, that it remained Christian during the period of the so-called Dark Ages, the Catholic mass being continuously celebrated since Roman times. The remarkable history of the Stonor family, who still live in the valley, provides a documented study for a period of over eight hundred years, which gives a profile of the area's history and the evolution of the landscape.

The Chiltern landscape – a designated Area of Outstanding Natural Beauty

---

Map 8 *The Chilterns*
A surprising amount of woodland remains to cover the chalk of the Chilterns. This is largely plantings of beech forest grown commercially here for many generations. The landscape still has an air of closeness and secrecy. Historians believe the Saxons never infiltrated the area and it remained an enclave of Christian British culture.

Based upon the 1984 Ordnance Survey 1:50,000 map with the permission of the Controller of Her Majesty's Stationery Office, Crown copyright reserved.

The family name Stonor comes from the nature of the land, 'stanare' meaning stony ground or ridge, doubtless a reference to the flints that abound in the chalk deposits. In Neolithic times these were mined for implements and even today are a characteristic building material.

Leland visited Stonor Park in 1538 when he described a 'fayre park and a warren of connes (rabbits) and fayre woods'.

A nineteenth-century visitor described his journey to Stonor Park: 'You wind along through undulating country within the sheltering hills, never seeing a mile or half a mile before you.'

The continuity of ownership of this part of South Oxfordshire by the Stonor family is one vital contributory factor in the appearance of the countryside today. Although successive centuries have seen a remorseless decline in the acreage under direct family control, the influence of family connections has resulted in the Stonor valley largely remaining in sizeable estate holdings. A similar pattern of large estates can be seen throughout a wide area of the Chilterns.

Ownership of land allows the exercise of the most direct form of management of the countryside. Although history provides many examples of some of the more bizarre eccentricities of taste and interest being given full rein in landscape design, the personal proclivities of landowners have usually been constrained by the economic necessities of land management. This is even more the case today.

Agriculture in the area has never entirely dominated the rural landscape of the Chilterns as it has in most parts of the English lowlands. Probably the sheep boom of the eighteenth century saw the greatest area of land given over to farming, particularly as the woodland cover had steadily diminished as general clearance went on. The thin flinty soils and steep slopes on the upper Chilterns were pretty hostile to the plough and the porous chalk geology could make water provision a problem. Many wells, often of great depth, were bored; some still survive from the Roman occupation. Elsewhere ponds were created by lining depressions in the chalk with clay.

The Hambleden valley was more favoured, having an almost perpetual bourn. Its waters today illustrate just how beautiful our river courses used to be; it looks, and is, good enough to drink. The Stonor valley has a 'woe' stream, so-called because legend says it only flows at times of strife.

Close to Upper Assendon farm is the 'war pond'. Recent history has helped to reinforce the legend. It filled in 1939 and partially in 1982 – the year of the Falklands war.

Generally, though, farmers in the area have needed to be skilful in their craft. Today the pattern is of very mixed husbandry and arable. There is no doubt farming has intensified but the wholesale clearance of landscape features such as hedgerows has been avoided. Traditional farm buildings are a considerable architectural heritage. For instance Upper Assendon Farm in the village of Stonor contains a magnificent example of a Chiltern barn complex.

Some of the tiny villages in the area have remained remarkably untouched, fitting into the countryside in an almost organic way. The use of flint, brick and locally produced tiles, and judicious planning of aspect and landscaping, all contribute to countryside of great quality. It is not surprising that the area is listed as one of Outstanding Natural Beauty.

Estate maps of 1765 show large areas of the Chilterns were owned by the Stonor family. Progressively the estate has been broken up and sold off

A reconstructed stone circle stands in front of Stonor House. Countless generations have lived in this valley

Above: The village of Hambleden, Bucks. Every effort has been made to conserve the original features and atmosphere of the community
Right: Spring brings a carpet of bluebells to the Chiltern beechwoods. The beechleaf has a translucent quality unique to British trees

Within the Chilterns for some centuries the varying fortunes of agriculture have been balanced by the economics of the other major land use – commercial woodland. Conventionally it is difficult to regard trees as a 'crop' like other plantings – and especially in the case of deciduous hardwoods – since their lifespan exceeds that of man. They are regarded more as permanent features of our environment than as an investment. This probably accounts for part of the emotional response to tree felling, many examples of which litter the verse of pastoral poets.

If the original natural forest cover was dominated by yew, thorn and juniper, it seems likely according to several accounts that man's influence led to a more mixed broadleaf forest with oak and beech being important elements. The demands for oak eventually favoured a domination by beech. This tree, with its shallow root system, seems to do particularly well in the thin chalky soils of the upper Chiltern slopes. For long periods a coppicing system provided for firewood needs with the various hardwoods being cut over every eight years or so.

At the beginning of the eighteenth century when agriculture generally was expanding at the expense of the woodlands, the Chilterns became a home for the furniture trade which grew steadily over the next two hundred years. The

Traditional woodland crafts now to be seen no more. Bodgers at their benches. They made kitchen furniture out of beech

favoured timber was beech and the woodland turner or bodger became a distinctive craftsman for the Chilterns. His work involved a forestry management system which became known as the Chiltern Selection System. Trees of various sizes were needed, and their felling allowed a mixed-age wood to develop with a fair degree of natural regeneration. The profitability of commercial beechwoods was now apparent, and the larger landowners who could countenance a long-term investment planted great acreages of beech. It is the results of such plantings we now see in many parts of the Chiltern countryside. Although greatly reduced, there is still a demand for beechwood. However, the past century has not seen an effective management policy with the result that many acres of beech are even aged and past their best. Several landowners are today faced with their crop of timber dying on its feet. This explains the clear felling of areas almost overnight – when a good market price can be got for the wood. Such dramatic changes have been rare in the Chilterns where the general appearance of the countryside has remained much the same for generations.

How can such a landscape have survived the pressures which have overwhelmed so many others? Is it purely accidental? Have the forces of commercial interest or of modern development somehow passed this area by,

Coppicing by the woodsman ensured suitable supplies of timber, and maintained a flourishing wildlife habitat

like the Saxon invaders of centuries ago? At first glance one may be tempted into thinking that this landscape is a testimony to a *laissez-faire* attitude to the countryside.

This is far from the truth. Indeed the closer analysis of this countryside reveals an adroit interlocking set of forces which, acting in concert, provide examples of highly dovetailed countryside management.

Today, as in past centuries, the influence of the landed gentry is still considerable over great areas of the countryside. This is certainly still the case in the Chilterns, and the Stonor and Hambleden valleys in particular. There is a permanence and durability about country society which must baffle a large section of our town-dwelling population. Some may argue that today's order of landowner, tenant farmer, and farm labourer, has more than a slight similarity to the hierarchy of Chaucer's time with its lord of the manor, yeoman farmer, and serf.

The continuity of title to large parts of the countryside has enabled landowners to pursue long-term management policies with their estates, and to influence through personal tastes the appearance and character of the rural scene.

Stonor Park remains today as a splendid landscaped park central to the valley. The fallow deer that roam the park are reminders of the Royal interest in hunting and Queen Victoria visited Stonor with the Royal Stag hounds in

With a life-span greater than man, the sudden clear-felling of stands of beech can produce emotional reactions

Stonor House and Park in the early 19th century. Remarkably little has changed today

1873. The passion for game shooting so enjoyed by the landed classes has also profoundly affected the appearance of the countryside. Cover in the form of woodlands, copses and hedgerows has been more assiduously guarded, even in the face of modern agricultural predations. A well-managed game shoot can be a profitable use for estate lands. The breeding of pheasants ensures adequate stocks for this expensive sport, whilst the susceptibility of partridge to agricultural chemicals is one contributory reason for some local land-owners discouraging their use on estate farms.

Nowadays even the largest estates find difficulty in maintaining both a balanced landscape and profitability. The unrelenting pursuit by the taxman of inherited wealth pushed many estates to the point of bankruptcy and break-up, or to adopt a policy of maximising their agricultural potential. Today, fortunately, there is some appreciation for the landscape contri-bution many estates do make to the diversity of the countryside. There are deeds of covenant which exempt landowners from some death duties and other tax arrangements could enable a more secure future for estates which remain as the more tangible evidence of our rural heritage.

The landed gentry have varied greatly in the expertise of their countryside management. Benign and farsighted barons have been succeeded by squandering heirs and the fortunes of estates have varied accordingly. Today the increasing trend is for landowners to employ the professional services of managing land agents. These trained and qualified technocrats now wield considerable influence in the countryside. Their corporate interest in land management and brokering combined with their considerable day-to-day influence over the running of estates enables them to influence strongly the countryside activities pursued and hence the appearance of the landscape.

The leasing arrangements for estate lands are varied and often complex. The freedom of action of tenant farmers can be almost total, on the one hand, with guaranteed tenure for himself and his successor, or it can be severely constrained by an annual leasing of land which the owner can take in hand or dispose of at will.

Both these extremes are found in the Stonor and Hambleden valleys. In addition certain farmers enjoy commons rights for grazing or other activities within the area. One common, Russell's Water and Maidensgrove, is now 'improved pasture' where little of the old herb-rich meadows survived wartime ploughing. It could revert to this if modern agricultural practices of fertilising and spraying were stopped, but the present agreement among farming commoners and the ever-increasing horse-riding fraternity seems to make this unlikely. Another common, at Summer Heath near Southend, is reverting to naturally regenerating mixed woodland as no agreement over commons rights has ever been achieved.

Nationally there is justifiable concern over the increasing loss of 'commons' and of the public's access to them. Since medieval times the process has been continuous, as private ownership has steadily appropriated the land of the commoner.

A home in this countryside is much in demand. The area has seen a considerable influx of prosperous individuals who have succeded in pricing up housing stock, from stately homes down to the humble cottage of the erstwhile bodger. The area is still home to long-established rural families but they have steadily lost ground to the invading commuters and those who see a rural environment conducive to their professions.

The newcomers have a strong vested interest in maintaining a high level of landscape amenity. Property investment is virtually a no risk venture and once ensconced the new country dweller devotes his energies to maintaining and enhancing his abode and to vociferous objection to any further development in the area. Little wonder then the area possesses one of the most influential amenity pressure groups in the Chiltern Society, who see the biggest problem as one of money. Agricultural land fetches about £2000 per hectare or £800 an acre, and building land fetches anything between about £200,000 per hectare or £80,000 an acre and £300,000 per hectare or £120,000 an acre. So there is a very strong incentive for developers. Formed in 1965, the Society has getting on for 4000 members, mostly individuals, but also 200 corporate members including local authorities, Parish Councils, residents' associations, civic societies, commercial firms and representatives of farming interests. They constitute what the society's literature claims is 'one of the largest and most influential amenity organisations in Great Britain' dedicated to 'encourage official and public interest in the conservation of the beauty, history and character of the Chiltern hills'. The society has a vociferous record in opposing a great range of developments adjudged detrimental to the amenity of the Chilterns and their efforts range from safeguarding footpaths and rights of way, to obstructing the building of motorways and ensuring the upkeep of archaeological monuments.

The society, as well as being firmly enmeshed into the political as well as the environmental fabric of the area, can also muster enough volunteer labour for more positive conservation projects when the need arises; woodland management and building restoration being favoured tasks. In 1965 the area was designated an Area of Outstanding Natural Beauty. This meant that the area was considered not only of local or regional significance but also of national importance.

Tucked away up a tributary valley to the Assendon (Stonor) Valley at Bix Bottom is the Warburg Nature Reserve. Its 106 hectares (263 acres) are administered by BBONT – the Berkshire, Buckinghamshire and Oxfordshire Naturalists' Trust. This reserve is the only one for which the trust maintains a full-time warden. The commonly-held view that all you do to create a nature reserve is to fence it and leave it alone is soon dispelled by witnessing the highly energetic management policy which is beginning to take shape. To a naturalist, the diversity of plant and animal life is the greatest achievement and these mixed areas of deciduous woodland and pasture are being turned into as diverse a microcosm of what the traditional habitats in the Chilterns must have once been.

The guidelines for the planner's view of such areas in the Chilterns are laid down in *A Plan for the Chilterns* published in 1971. This outline of planning intent was the expression of what was deemed a desirable policy by the Chiltern standing conference – a committee formed in 1967 by the County Councils of Bedfordshire, Buckinghamshire, Hertfordshire and Oxfordshire with other members from the Countryside Commission, Nature Conservancy and the National Trust.

The preface to the plan outlines its pragmatic philosophy. It maintains that 'The policies must provide for the conservation of the Chilterns not only to make a contribution for leisure pursuits but also to allow the ecology of the area to evolve in its own peculiar way. It must remain a living area where forestry and farming can be carried on in a robust and confident manner.'

The perceived pressures on the area are ominously but rather vaguely expressed in a rising scale of population figures. Living within the designated Area of Outstanding Natural Beauty (AONB) there is a population of 80,000; within three kilometres (two miles) however are 542,000 and within

40 kilometres (25 miles) $8\frac{1}{2}$ million. Such a huge reservoir of potential demand for development of all kinds leads at times to a rather siege-like mentality where constant vigilance is required to man the barricades of statutory planning.

From the brief outline of the interests of the major organised influences on the landscape of the Stonor and Hambleden valleys it becomes clear that there is a good deal in common. The countryside which has evolved is highly regarded by most of the groups who see by and large a sympathetic understanding of their own interests by others.

It is of interest for example to hear that the planners of South Oxfordshire District Council believe they have enough statutory powers to resist any untoward changes in the fabric of the countryside. Indeed in some instances they have chosen not to apply powers they have, but to rely on negotiation.

Members of the Chiltern Society keep a close eye on a wide range of developments and are strong enough to have bargained for a considerable amount of official consultation which keeps planners on their toes.

Local landowners act as a constraining force on the farmers, whilst the naturalists, although genuinely concerned about the wider countryside, benefit from local patronage to pursue their conservation policies within the nature reserves.

This part of the British countryside some may argue shows what can be conserved when a balance of interests prevails rather than any one land use view gaining dominance. Such a balance is rare for most parts of the British countryside where all too often one land use interest is dominant. How such interests more generally exercise their power politically is a subject to which we turn next.

Left: The winter landscape of Stonor Park

Chapter II
Politics of Change

IN 1970, Max Nicholson, who had long served as chairman of the government's Nature Conservancy Council, wrote: 'It can be said with some confidence that the 1970s will mark the first moments in man's tenure of the earth when the nature of the conduct of his stewardship will be continuously under critical scientific scrutiny, not too far separated from the seats of power and from the enforcement of accountability.' But, as this book has shown, the countryside in England and Wales has taken such a severe buffeting as a result of powerful social and economic forces that his forecast has been very wide of the mark. Perhaps his misjudgement stems from an innate optimism in science and its ability to solve problems and a belief that the ultimate truth of such solutions must gain acceptance.

Unfortunately, as any social scientist will tell you, the reality is different; anyone who believes that what happens in the countryside is only a result of social and economic forces rather than which pressure groups have direct access to the political machine is engaging in self-delusion. Indeed, the effectiveness of controls on landscape change merely tells one about the strengths and weaknesses of the participants who attempt to influence the development of legislation relating to rural matters. This legislation speaks of the comparative success of those who exploit the rural environment for their own economic ends. Indeed, especially effective in bending the ear of governments have been the farmers and landowners, as compared to environmentalists who have tried to promote an attitude which recognises the rural environment not simply as an exploitable economic resource but as an integral and almost sacred part of man's heritage in which all must share equally. This is to make no political or moral judgement about either group but merely to establish a major, albeit rough, generalisation. Indeed, when taxed with the accusation that he is destroying the countryside, the agribusinessman would reply that he is merely doing what the law allows him to do and current subsidies and grants encourage him to do. This, of course, is true, although it skates over the fact that such farmers have been remarkably adept at persuading successive governments of their own point of view. And they have achieved this through the activities of two organisations which represent their interests: the National Farmers' Union (NFU) and the Country Landowners' Association (CLA).

Numerous political analysts consider it irrefutable that the NFU is by far the most successful lobbying group in Britain. Founded in 1908 to counter

The beginning of a formidable partnership. National Farmers' Union delegation leaves No. 10 Downing Street after post-war discussions on the future of British agriculture

the threat of organised labour in the farming industry, it now boasts a membership of two-thirds of all farmers. But its real success stems from the post-war period when its interests were carried along on a tide of enthusiasm for what agriculture had achieved during the war in terms of the United Kingdom feeding itself, and it was felt that if a high level of self-sufficiency could be sustained at a time of economic stringency, much would be contributed to our balance of payments. It was no small wonder that the NFU was able to negotiate a formal seat with government at the table at which farm prices and guarantees would be established each year. Since then its 'behind the scenes' success in having the ear of the Minister and the officials of the Ministry of Agriculture, Fisheries and Food has been remarkable – to the extent that the relationship with this government department may be described now as symbiotic. As Howard Newby has neatly summarised it: 'The ministry needs the NFU in order to have a representative organisation to negotiate with, one which can deliver its membership on any agreed deal over prices and guarantees. The presence of the NFU also enables the ministry to sound out farming opinion on any issue before developing a definite policy matter. Similarly, the NFU needs the ministry, without which it would lose much of its *raison d'être*. It provides the NFU with a direct channel of influence into even the highest government circles.'[30] The value of such an intimate relationship cannot be under-estimated; it has fostered the belief that farmers are the best custodians of the countryside and its ultimate economic viability, and that little or nothing need be done in terms of formal structures or counterbalancing controls in this respect. The fact that planning controls have never been applied to farming is a working testament to the acceptance of the NFU view in government circles.

But more than having the ear of government itself, the NFU has also assiduously courted Members of Parliament as well as the elected members of local government of all parties, thus enhancing its effectiveness as a lobbying machine. In the Houses of Parliament it has full-time liaison officers handing on information relevant to NFU interests and services an All-Party Committee on Agriculture. At local level it negotiates in areas of rural planning and countryside access. Also, within a wider framework, the NFU is a master of the public relations game. It has been reported that in 1975 alone it issued 162 national press notices, held 12 major press conferences, sent out 8000 press releases to local newspapers, placed 200 special articles and was involved in 100 local radio programmes. In each week the NFU monitoring service was able to record 1200 references to it on radio and television involving no less than 31 hours of broadcasting. As Newby has concluded, 'If we consider the post-war history of agriculture then it is not only the government of the day but the NFU which has been responsible for guiding and shaping the destiny of the majority of British farmers.' And he might have also added that it has thereby succeeded in controlling and shaping much of what has happened in and to the countryside of England and Wales over that period.

Almost equally effective in looking after the interests of landowners, as opposed to farmers alone, has been the Country Landowners' Association founded in 1907. Well aware that the idea of large landowners forming a trade union could be a political anathema it has in recent years encouraged the membership of very small landowners (fifty per cent of its members now own under a hundred acres) and at the same time pursued its cause quietly down the corridors of power, giving special attention to 'behind-the-scenes' consultations with Whitehall civil servants. As its literature maintains, CLA leaders 'have direct access to ministers and Head Office permanent staff have a close day-to-day working relationship with government departments'.

Many of its activities involve getting the best deal possible from the Chancellor of the Exchequer over taxation matters, though its involvement with environmental issues has recently been much more to the fore insofar as it has made the point that high environmental standards of estate manage-

The traditional meet of the foxhounds: still a common, if now more controversial, sight in the countryside where landowners exert enormous influence on the appearance of the landscape

ment should carry less punitive levels of taxation – particularly on the death of the owner. Especially important here have been its attempts to avoid punitive (as the CLA would describe them) levels of Capital Transfer Tax which it believes could ultimately lead to the demise of the private landlord. As Newby has said, 'If the private landowner has become adept at avoiding his long predicted oblivion, this has been in no small part due to the CLA's political guile.'

Although it has a strong regional network with sixty-seven county branches, the most decisive channel of influence remains the one between its London HQ and Whitehall and Westminster. Whilst it may like to maintain that it has a non-political stance in dealings at that level and avoids overtly playing its hand in the public gaze, the strength of its membership on the Conservative benches of the two Houses of Parliament should not be overlooked.

Ranged against these two powerful independent pressure groups and promoting an opposing viewpoint are the small *conservationist* bodies – many of which are really effective only at a level which is divorced from that of directly influencing the policymakers. This is in no way to denigrate organisations that set their sights no higher than opposing what they consider to be specifically damaging to the countryside. An eminently successful group by the standards of such organisations is the Friends of the Lake District, now celebrating its fiftieth birthday. This has resisted afforestation, bypasses, firing ranges, power boats on the lakes, and many other examples of what it considers to be incompatible intrusions in a national park.

But perhaps a better example of this kind of organisation is to be found at national level in the Royal Society for Nature Conservation (RSNC) which is in fact an umbrella group bringing together the forty-two county Naturalists' Trusts. It began life as a group attempting to persuade the National Trust to purchase nature reserves, but when it failed to do so, it set about raising money to acquire its own, a pursuit at which it has been singularly good. A very much larger organisation, the Royal Society for the Protection of Birds, has a more specific remit than the conservation of the countryside, though of late its concern for the destruction of habitats has been a major preoccupation. Whilst again not having a direct influence in high places, both it and the RSNC have recently done much to canvass public support for wildlife conservation.

Whilst avoiding the temptation to list all the organisations which fall into this category, it is probably fair to say that the only conclusive evidence of national 'clout' happened when a number of these came together for the first time under the chairmanship of Lord Melchett to oppose the passage of the 1981 Wildlife and Countryside Bill. Calling itself Wildlife Link it acted as a spokesbody for over twenty diverse voluntary organisations. As Charles Pye-Smith and Chris Rose have agreed, 'There is no doubt that their united front added much strength to the campaign to force the government to produce an improved piece of legislation.'[31] Moreover, it seems almost certain that it was important in persuading the Labour Party to adopt its new avowed policy of extending planning controls to agricultural and forestry activities.

But even the most successful of the environmental groups, the Council for the Protection of Rural England (CPRE), with a record of having fought for many important causes including the campaigns to have legislation for national parks and AONBs on the statute book, is only an *influencing* group. Its success depends on it marshalling support for its causes and convincing others of the rightness of its point of view. It differs markedly from the NFU and CLA which are, of course, more than just pressure groups since they represent clearly identifiable and homogeneous sectors of society. As Andrew Coleman has put it, 'They tend more often than not to be able to engage in genuine bargaining than do purely promotional or cause groups which do not speak for any specific interest other than society at large.'

It is hardly surprising then that the interests of farmers and landowners have remained paramount, in spite of a wide range of legislation which attempts to protect the environment, and small wonder that the government agencies responsible for such protection lack both legislative support and the financial resources to impose their will. Rather, they exist in the hope that coming to terms with the forces affecting change will achieve the ends they seek. Of the two organisations concerned, the 1981/2 budget for the Nature Conservancy Council (NCC) was £10 million and that of the Countryside Commission (CC), £2 million. This may be compared with £5000 million spent on agricultural support in the same year. As Charles Pye-Smith and Chris Rose have remarked the projected £8000 million to be spent on the Trident nuclear missile programme is 'equivalent to eight centuries of state conservation at present prices'. This is not, of course, to suggest that the organisations concerned have not done their utmost within the framework in which they are forced to work. The Countryside Commission's former director, the late Reg Hookway, commented upon this very point. He has said that 'everything we have achieved in protecting the environment has been by dint of fighting the combined opposition of vested interests'.

However, critics are increasingly asking whether the will to oppose will remain with such organisations. In 1971 Malcolm MacEwen, in listening to an

Left: Forerunner of most of the modern conservation groups, the Council for the Preservation of Rural England supported a number of important campaigns even before the Second World War. *Right*: Many countryfolk still resent their town-dwelling cousins; their fears are reflected in a pre-war *Punch* cartoon. *Mrs Hawkins*: ''AVE A GOOD LOOK ROUND, BERT, AND SEE THAT WE 'AVEN'T LEFT ANYTHINK.'

Conservation volunteers pollarding in a Nature Reserve at Stodmarsh, Kent. Such work maintains a diverse habitat for wildlife

One of the many conservation areas sponsored by County Naturalist Trusts. These are often tiny enclaves of the countryside

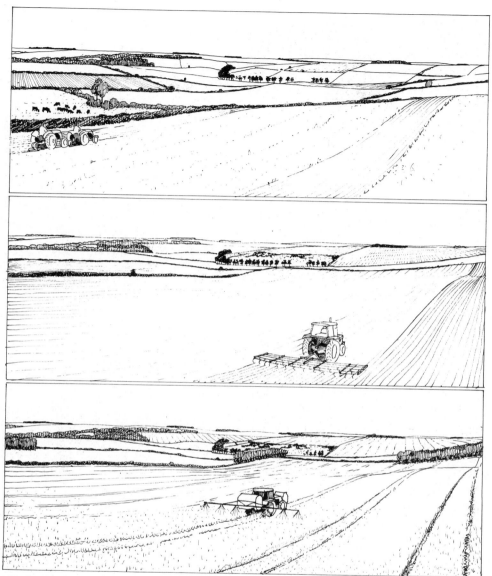

Through its New Agricultural Landscapes project the Countryside Commission attempts to ameliorate the impact of new farming methods on the landscape. The middle picture shows what can be lost from the landscape shown at the top. The bottom picture indicates how landscape can be improved with only a modest outlay

address to the National Parks Conference from Ralph Verney, wrote that 'he laid so much stress on the priority to be given to the production of food, the needs of the hill farmer, the production of timber and the extraction of minerals that I was left wondering whether the national parks enjoyed in his eyes any specific protection at all. He was opposed to any form of additional controls over farming and forestry, echoing the Scott Committee (1944) in saying that the farmer seeks not to destroy the landscape but to enhance it.'[32] It might seem strange to some that a person with such views could subsequently be appointed to chair the government's wildlife agency, the NCC, though many interpreters of the move, including Christopher Hall, former director of the CPRE, are in no doubt that 'it owed much to direct lobbying by the CLA and NFU'. Since then, William Williamson has been appointed to this post, and his background is that of a farmer and businessman. There has also been an apparent shift on its Council, which has filled a number of conservation groups with alarm, from a body largely served by naturalists and ecologists, to one dominated by landowning interests. Of course this is a legitimate move by the government of the day but as a not entirely disinterested commentator recently put it, 'We would not suggest that the Ministry of Agriculture or the Department of Energy should be run by conservationists; by the same token we do not believe that farmers and foresters should be asked to run the NCC or CC.'

In conclusion, one could say that since 1945 the state's policy on the countryside has been much influenced by pressure groups representing farmers and landowners which mainly promote agricultural interests. This was broadly accepted by the public until the late 1960s and 1970s. Then it was realised, especially by conservationists, that new agricultural techniques coupled with the levels of support for farming, particularly for arable farming after Britain joined the EEC, meant that farmers could no longer claim to be the custodians of the countryside. But such has been the power of their lobby that conservation interest groups have as yet been unable to challenge effectively a now entrenched agricultural system. They have found themselves in a situation where the government arms of conservation, the NCC and the CC, are caught up in a battle against those with resources of manpower and finance they cannot hope to match but who are bringing about unparalleled changes in the countryside.

It is in fact a totally unequal struggle, compounded, so the conservationists would say, by a Wildlife and Countryside Act (1981) which has had the effect of permitting farmers to claim compensation from those already under-funded conservancy agencies for *not* undertaking agricultural activities which would harm particularly sensitive environments. Unfortunately for the NCC and the CC the possibilities of other direct action to head off such situations seems even more limited. Given their budgets, it is legitimate to question the number of nature reserves that they might be able to purchase outright when the going rate for agricultural land is so high. Even the National Trust is now having to accept its inability to conserve through direct purchase and relies increasingly on the acceptance of new properties as gifts. But even in such cases, some guarantee of future financial help in the

St Michael's Mount, Cornwall. One of the many properties the National Trust could only accept on condition that financial support for its upkeep was available from the former owners

management and upkeep of these is usually required, in spite of an income that approaches £30 million a year. However, it should also be remembered that there are other forces at work effecting change that conservation agencies need to take account of. For instance, those changes created by the continuance of the road-building programme earnestly pressed upon the government by the influential transport lobby, and in and around the national parks the demands made for afforestation, mineral extraction, water collection and even power generation. Fortunately, where these other forms of potential development are concerned, they are subject to planning controls, unlike agriculture, and in this respect contentious development proposals are bound to go to a public inquiry. This at least offers an opportunity not only for all interest groups to put their case publicly but for the private citizen to feed in his or her own personal views for ultimate evaluation by the inspector and inclusion in his report to the Secretary of State for the Environment, the ultimate decision-maker.

So the questions that remain are therefore twofold; can anything be done to redress the balance between conservation and other resource-based interests, especially agriculture, which make demands on the countryside, and if so, what realistically *will* be done?

Chapter 12
Future Landscapes

 THE responses to that question, which asks whether anything can or should be done to redress the balance between conservation and other resource-based interests, especially agriculture, have taken many forms. Not surprisingly, agricultural interests favour little more than window-dressing for the good of their public image or what the *Farmers Weekly* has recently described, somewhat dismissively, as 'fitting conservation into a busy farm'. This, they would maintain, should be done through the local Farming and Wildlife Advisory Groups (FWAG) which originated in 1969 when a group of conservationists first got together to discuss wildlife protection with farmers, representatives from MAFF, the NFU and the CLA. Groups based on this original concept now exist in every county in England and Wales and a number have full-time officers who advise interested farmers on conservation. Apart from image building, its promoters see FWAG as an important advisory system which can provide valuable information on free conservation services as well as the availability of grants. However, its entirely voluntary nature means that many of those responsible for major changes in the rural landscape are the very ones most

New colours in the countryside. A field of oilseed rape flowers in the Berkshire landscape. Lurid yellow shocks the eye

Conservation advice to farmers is available from Farming and Wildlife Advisory Groups. There is one in every county

likely to ignore the opportunities it offers. This has left it wide open to criticism from those who would espouse a cause other than that put by the farming lobby and hope to find a solution which deals more even-handedly with conservation interests. The mildest of such reformers see an answer in the amalgamation of the NCC and the CC. This would not only replace what many believe to be the unique British absurdity of having one organisation looking after nature and the other amenity and landscape, but provide additional strength in such unity. Bryn Green, formerly an NCC regional officer and now of Wye College, has argued strongly in his book *Countryside Conservation* that such an amalgamation would certainly enable them to tackle effectively for the first time those sectors of government responsible for the agricultural support system policy. Others (including Malcolm and Ann MacEwen) believe that this can and should merely act as a prelude to a recognition by government that conservation must be structured into the entire apparatus of subsidies, grants and tax incentives relating to agriculture and to forestry. Such a suggestion, however, takes the discussion into a whole field of new policies and policy alternatives that have been put forward both by individuals and groups. Since these deserve detailed attention they can for this purpose best be considered in three distinctive categories.

First, there are those who believe that the conservation problem could be ameliorated in the short term by quite modest alterations in current policies that would be relatively simple to enact through legislation in Parliament. Then there are those who suggest new and more radical approaches that are not necessarily difficult to put into action, requiring again only legislative restructuring, but do involve a major shift in political if not public opinion. It would be unlikely therefore that they could be brought about in the short or even the medium term. Finally, there are those who put forward highly-imaginative scenarios that may only be seen as very long-term approaches, distant visions, if you like, of a new rural 'promised land'.

Of the first group, two main factions have so far appeared. One of these suggests that much of the damage to the rural environment currently being created could be remedied by the imposition of planning controls on the main agents of destruction: farming and forestry. This is the scenario most favoured by the conservationists, who would argue that it would be a relatively simple matter to impose such constraints upon the rather small number of people who own land and use it. Unless this is done and done

The exemption of farming from many planning controls can result in new buildings that dominate the rural landscape

quickly, we will be unable to stave off the threat to Sites of Special Scientific Interest (SSSIs) and Nature Reserves which the present Wildlife and Countryside Act cannot hope to protect, so the group argues. As already noted the overall sums from which compensation is available to farmers for *not* destroying such sites are insufficient should a large number of these become threatened. Indeed Christopher Hall, former director of the CPRE, has pointed to the absurdity of a situation in which farmers can be compensated for losses that they have never really sustained. 'If farmers are to be paid for these notional losses then by the same token the ordinary citizen refused planning permission to add a garage to his semi-detached ought to be able to claim compensation for the loss of the value to his property,'[33] Hall has argued. But perhaps the chief advocate of this solution has been Marion Shoard whose arguments have been most effectively put in her book *The Theft of the Countryside*.

Whilst not rejecting the Shoard scenario others with conservation close to their hearts have argued that a stronger case exists for getting to the root economic cause of the destruction of the countryside – the farmers' subsidy-induced prosperity. As John Bowers and Paul Cheshire have put it, 'We have chosen to subsidise precisely those activities – the use of artificial fertilisers, hedgerow removal, land drainage etc. – which cause the damage to a real resource [the countryside]. And these damage-causing activities are already financially rewarded by farm support prices. Farmers have been subsidised twice over to despoil the rural environment.'[34] The trouble at present, according to Bowers and Cheshire, is that amenity is under-priced by comparison with food production since it is impossible to charge consumers directly for amenity. Hence there is what economists call market failure. The solution, they argue, is either to tax the farmer for providing agricultural output by environmentally damaging techniques or to subsidise forms of production which conserve the environment.

However, if the objective is to save both the natural heritage as well as the social fabric of the countryside, a third option is available – that of land reform. Although this is a more extreme solution, if not in the same class as state control of land through nationalisation, a suggestion put forward by the agricultural workers branch of the Transport and General Workers' Union, this envisages the introduction of a land tax or the state ownership of ground rent. Robert Waller, a leading exponent of this approach, has suggested that such a tax should distinguish between natural resources beneath and upon the land, and wealth produced by labour and capital.

By separating what nature has created (land and natural resources) from what man has produced (houses, quarries, mines, factories, farms etc.) we can lay the foundations of a new economic order that safeguards

Highly productive, but virtually void of wildlife interest. The Hampshire Curves

enterprise from being seized by the state without depriving the state of its past share in the community wealth; for the wealth created on any site is partly the fruit of the labour of those who work on it and partly the consequence of the prosperity of the community as a whole. Thus the community has of right a share in the wealth produced on its land. If such rights are secured by a variable tax related to the value of the site, it clearly could not be held speculatively. The occupier of the site could not afford to leave it inactive since he could not pay the rent and land would become more equitably distributed. Land would only be left alone and people excluded from certain forms of industrial enterprise when it was what the community wanted, perhaps to deploy it for conservation and amenity. In such an instance the occupier of the site would be exempted from the land tax.[35]

Whilst such reforms may seem simple enough in their execution, it is clear that before implementation, and indeed during it, it would be necessary to find a way of discovering what the community wants to do with the land, an exercise perhaps best undertaken in most instances at local government level. However, a difficulty would remain in the use of areas such as National Parks where local priorities would need to be weighed against national ones. But even more difficult would be the problem of politically creating a climate in which the community, rather than the individual, effectively determines what happens to land.

The third group of alternative scenarios, those that can only be achieved in the long term, consist of a number of relatively disparate ideas. This is an inevitable consequence of 'futurology' where the imagination can roam more freely, unfettered by constraints. However, there is some common ground amongst those who would advocate a change to a mode of farming based on a low-energy, high-labour input approach with a switch in the application of public money to environmentally sensitive activities.

Charles Secrett of the Friends of the Earth has advocated such an approach stressing the lack of reason in current policies which merely bring more land into use, which results in the production of excessive quantities of food for which there is no demand. He calls instead for a change to farming practices in harmony with the environment such as coppicing woodland, the construction of dry-stone walls and the planting of hedges, stock limitations on and the fencing of sensitive moor and heathlands. He also demands income support for those who serve such conservation ends. The consumption of petrochemicals as a fertiliser, he believes, must be abandoned in favour of natural organic fertilisers, thus reducing health hazards. Equally, these must not be used for energy where biomass and solar sources can be

The demand for minerals continues to eat into the countryside: a limestone quarry in the Mendip Hills

substituted. He calls for a countryside which is not a living museum or a food factory but 'an environment supporting as wide a variety of occupations, habitats, wild species and people as possible', words that might almost have been taken from the introduction to the guide to the Parc National des Cévennes.

The ideas of Secrett have been developed to more extreme levels by John Seymour, Anthony Farmer, Konrad Smigelski and others who see 'the only alternative to capital-intensive, labour-free, large-scale farming as small-scale, labour-intensive farming'. They believe such reformed productive systems will not result in a reduction but a four- or five-fold increase in food output and that they will be sustained by processes which avoid 'the present system of the mechanical and chemical rape of the soil fostered by the Ministry of Agriculture'. As with the Secrett camp, organic farming would be at the heart of the production process, perhaps with such farms associated with self-supporting co-operative villages.

If the key to this approach is high levels of production but from small intensive units which are environmentally acceptable, one alternative would be to maintain the notion of intensive production but promote it to the nth degree by every method known to agricultural science. These units could produce so much that relatively small numbers of them would be required to fulfil the need for home-produced food. Considerations of this kind

Another prairie – this time in Oxfordshire – affords a clear view of another modern intrusion into the countryside: Didcot Power Station

inevitably take us towards the more extreme futuristic scenarios. But at least one person, Roger Grimley of Velcourt Ltd (a well-known consortium of agribusinessmen), has provided a clear picture of what such units would be like. To begin with they would be in blocks of around 2000 hectares (under 5000 acres) and located on prime soils. Only movable windbreaks would separate fields. High-energy-yielding crops only would be grown. Cereals would be cultivated for humans and animal feed with starch converted to sugar and alcohol and straw into feed. Legumes would be produced as protein and rape for oils; root crops would be raised only where they were high in sugar for human use and conversion to alcohol. Grass would be produced but for direct feeding to animals which would be entirely housed. Every part of the operation would be computer-controlled so that fertilisers and pesticides and irrigation water could be supplied via pipelines, at the correct moment, having monitored climate and soil conditions. Harvesting would also take place when optimum circumstances had been determined, but in this respect these farms would be so located as to make the best use of prevailing climatic conditions. Farms in the eastern part of the country would grow cereals, legumes and roots, while those in the west would treat grass as a crop using arable methods.

Although there is more to the highly-intensive technological approach than it is possible to consider here, the important point is that these

Organic fertilisers, a useful by-product of traditional mixed farming. Many believe that their use is important to safeguard the health of the soil in the long term

techniques not only produce all that is required efficiently, but they would permit all the truly marginal farm land, which is also more often than not in those areas of greatest potential scenic beauty, to be given over 'to leisure pursuits, the conservation of wildlife with enhanced facilities for public access and enjoyment'.[36] Only the prime agricultural land would be retained for food production.

Of course most of the scenarios for the future of the countryside are inevitably geared towards the maintenance of an acceptable rural environment, meaning that of the open country rather than the village. But where the village is concerned, such notions as self-sufficiency, co-operation, local action, the pooling of resources including built space and common ownership all loom large. This is because advocates of the village of tomorrow are all too mindful of the need to avoid the social and economic inequities of its contemporary counterparts. Therefore they look to the new village as a community which will be large enough to embrace many skills and to justify a range of communual services, but small enough to be comprehended as a social unit by those who live there. What is obvious is that such a model lies at a total remove from the commuter-dominated village that is so much a part of lowland England and Wales. And yet the studies of Dartington Institute in particular concerning the utopian future for the village community at least accept and reconcile the two most important revolutions which have occurred in the late twentieth century – the 'green' or ecological movement and the micro-electronic era.

However, to return to the main theme of this discussion, it is obvious that only those conservation ideas which require modest changes to current legislation are likely to be embraced in the immediate future. But which of those suggestions which make up our first group of scenarios, if any, might be considered a front runner can only be a matter of enlightened conjecture. Enlightened, because there is evidence, in the working of the Wildlife and Countryside Act for example, that the government which passed it through to the statute book is developing an ethos of reaching agreement in influencing the countryside environment rather than invoking control. Equally, we know that the opposition Labour Party had a commitment in their last election manifesto to extend planning controls to encompass agricultural and forestry activities. But even though there is a strong association between the Conservative Party and farming and land economy interests and we are aware of the power and strength of the NFU and the CLA as effective lobbies compared with conservation groups, the winds of policy change may well be beginning to blow inside Cabinet. Undoubtedly the costs of the recent policy of agricultural support (some £5000 million in 1983) is proving so financially crippling and so money-gobbling of funds that are needed for other European Community projects that a Conservative minister of agriculture has already agreed to a withdrawal (albeit a limited one) of some support for dairying. It will be evident enough that any fall in commodity production subsidies or other forms of agricultural assistance are bound to take the pressure off further plans to expand or to intensify production.

Yet against this one can only note other countervailing forces. Earlier attempts by the NCC to protect the Somerset Levels against agricultural improvement, much to the anger of local farmers, came to nothing after the appointment of its present chairman in 1983. Moreover, the recent establishment of the European Environment Fund by the EEC was not only opposed by the British Government, but when it had been set up, it did its best to ensure that it was minimally funded.

Nevertheless, it is possible to say that there is a rising tide of awareness about what is happening to the countryside other than that disseminated by the NFU. Radio and television, in response to popular demand, have whole series of programmes related to ecology and conservation as well as living in the countryside. To cite but one particularly popular programme, an average of nine million watch *Wildlife on One*, whilst audience research has indicated that amongst the programmes shown on both BBC channels those concerning wildlife elicit the highest levels of satisfaction. Apart from regular series, special programmes on the impact of agribusiness on the rural

A camera crew filming the Nature Conservancy Council's mud pump in action at Ranworth Reserve, Norfolk. Television has stimulated public concern

environment have appeared with increasing regularity in the last two years. *Harvest Gold* from ITV created such a furore in the farming press because of its even-handed approach to agriculture and conservation that correspondence about it rumbled on throughout the summer of 1983. The newspapers also provide ample coverage and the *Observer* now has a regular 'Save Our Countryside' article each week. Books from John Bowers and Paul Cheshire, from Marion Shoard, from Richard Mabey and from Richard Body (making a case not dissimilar to that of Bowers and Cheshire) have all been influential with their arguments explored in articles and broadcast discussions elsewhere. But whatever causes they may espouse, and they are largely polemical in tone, they have pushed forward people's awareness of the changes taking place in the countryside today and their root cause, which really when it comes down to it is one of a conflict of interests in a country which has very limited space and a large population. As the Duke of Edinburgh recently wrote,

> To the farmer and the forester (the prime users of the countryside) it is a source of income; to the extractor of minerals it is a part of an industrial process; to builders and manufacturers it is a place for houses and factories; to the transport industries it is a place to build roads, canals, railways, airports and harbours; to the energy industries it is a place for power stations, dams and refineries; to the leisure industry it is a place for sport and recreation; to the casual visitor it is all too often a place to drop rubbish before going home; to wild animals and plants it is home.[37]

No attempts at a reconciliation of these disparate vested interests can ever be easy and certainly none of the scenarios put forward in this chapter can make all of these groups equally happy. The best any one of them might claim is that it moved in the direction of applying a greater degree of evenhandedness between the groups. As for this book its authors would make no greater claim for it than that it should shed light on the nature of these conflicting interests, leaving you to make up your mind about how we might best try to conserve those aspects of the countryside that are of real value.

References

1   W. G. Hoskins, *The Making of the English Landscape*, Penguin, Harmondsworth, 1977
2   Nan Fairbrother, *New Lives, New Landscapes*, Penguin, Harmondsworth, 1972
3   Marion Shoard, *Theft of the Countryside*, Maurice Temple Smith, London, 1982
4   Richard Mabey, *The Common Ground*, Hutchinson, London, 1980
5   H. C. Darby, *The Domesday Geography of Eastern England*, Cambridge University Press, 1971
6   John Britton with E. W. Brayley, *The Beauties of England & Wales*, Vernor & Hood, London, 1801–15 (Delineations of each country)
7   Flora Thompson, *Lark Rise to Candleford*, Penguin, Harmondsworth, 1973
8   George Borrow, *Wild Wales*, Murray, London, 1907
9   Ann and Malcolm MacEwen, *National Parks : Conservation or Cosmetics?* Allen & Unwin, London, 1981
10   Roy Millward & Adrian Robinson, *The Landscapes of North Wales*, David & Charles, Newton Abbot, 1978
11   Miss Spence, *Patterdale Past and Present* (unpublished), 1933
12   *A Study of the Hartsop Valley : a report to the Countryside Commission and the Lake District Special Planning Board* prepared during 1975 by Rural Planning Services Ltd, Countryside Commission, Cheltenham, 1976 (CCP:92)
13   Howard Hill, *Freedom to Roam*, Moorland, Ashbourne, 1980
14   *Manchester Guardian*, 21 April 1925
15   A. C. Todd and Peter Laws, *The Industrial Archaeology of Cornwall*, David & Charles, Newton Abbot, 1972
16   Friedrich Engels, *The Conditions of the English Working Class*, Allen & Unwin, London, 1968
17   *Children Employment Commission Reports*
18   J. A. Paris, *Guide to the Mounts Bay*, Gough, London, 1824
19   A. G. Folliott-Stokes, *Cornish Coast and Moors*, Greaning & Co., London, 1912
20   John Barr, *Derelict Britain*, Penguin, Harmondsworth, 1970
21   Jack Clemo, *My Cornwall*, Bossiney Books, St Teath, 1973
22   Daphne du Maurier, *Vanishing Cornwall*, Gollancz, London, 1981
23   Jack Clemo, *The Two Beds* in *Penguin Modern Poets 6*, Penguin, Harmondsworth, 1964
24   Peggy Pollard, *Vision of England : Cornwall*, Paul Elek, London, 1947
25   John Hadfield, *The Shell Book of English Villages*, Michael Joseph, London, 1980
26   Wesley Dougill, *The English Coast : Its Development and Preservation*, Council for the Preservation of Rural England, The Council, London, 1936
27   Bryn Green, *Countryside Conservation*, Allen & Unwin, London, 1980
28   E. A. Ellis, *The Broads*, New Naturalist Series, Collins, London, 1965
29   C. S. Middlelow, *The Broadland Photographers*, Albion Books, Norwich, 1982
30   Howard Newby, *Green and Pleasant Land*? Penguin, Harmondsworth, 1980
31   Charles Pye-Smith and Chris Rose, *Crisis and Conservation*, Penguin, Harmondsworth, 1984
32   Malcolm MacEwen, *Future Landscapes*, Chatto & Windus, London, 1976
33   Christopher Hall, 'The Amenity Movement', in C. Gill (ed.), *The Countryman's Britain*, David & Charles, Newton Abbot, 1976
34   John Bowers and Paul Cheshire, *Agriculture, the Countryside and Land Use ; an Ecomomic Critique*, Methuen, London, 1983
35   Robert Waller, in Girardet, H. (ed.), *Land for the People*, Crescent Books, London, 1976
36   Robert Grimley, in *The Changing Countryside*, editors John Blunden and Nigel Curry, Croom Helm, London, 1985
37   Duke of Edinburgh, 'Save Our Countryside', *The Observer*, 20 May 1984

Index

Page numbers in *italic* refer to illustrations.